French Cooking
simplified with a
Food Processor

by Ruth Howse

block cuts by
Rik Olson

101 Productions
San Francisco

Dedicated with love to my husband Paul
and my children Paula and Forrest

Third Printing, April 1979

Printed and bound in the United States of America.

Distributed to the book trade in the United States
by Charles Scribner's Sons, New York

Published by 101 Productions
834 Mission Street
San Francisco, California 94103

Library of Congress Cataloging in Publication Data
Howse, Ruth
    French cooking simplified with a food processor.

    Includes index.
    1.   Cookery, French.   2.   Food processor
cookery.   I.   Title.
TX719.H63   641.5'89   77-13150
ISBN 0-89286-129-0

Contents

Introduction

Those who know how to eat are comparatively ten years younger than those to whom this art is unknown.
　　　　　　　　　　　　　　　　　　　　　　　　　　　　　　　—Brillat-Savarin

It is said that whether it be business or pleasure, all in France begins *à la table.* The prominent role of food in French culture stems from ancient tradition; in spite of the many demands of the modern world, the meal is still the nucleus of family life. This ritual is taken most seriously, and on occasion a meal can easily last as long as four hours.

French cuisine encompasses a variety of regional differences and therein lies its success. Normandy is justly renowned for its creamy butter and rich cream. These, often with Calvados, go into the preparation of some of the most famous French sauces. Brittany, in spite of poor soil, grows some of the best vegetables in the country, Breton artichokes leading the long list. Fish and seafood are also abundant in this sea-bordered province. Périgord is the land of truffles, which go into the preparation of delicious pâtés and other dishes. Provence gave to French cuisine many aromatic herbs; olive oil and garlic also characterize a "Provençal" dish. Alsace contributed its marvelous sausages. Burgundy does infinite justice to its wines by incorporating them into a variety of dishes. Its vineyards also yield a most prized by-product, those escargots, which cooked in butter and herb sauce simply melt in your mouth. Throughout the centuries these regional cuisines have crossbred to create the marvelously diverse cuisine of France.

When planning a French menu, a number of factors must be considered. Dishes served should complement one another in flavor and texture and should progress from lighter to richer foods. The raw ingredients you select should be nutritious and of high quality. Seasonal availability, and consequently cost, should also guide your decisions. Finally, the menu will vary according to the purpose—whether the meal is to be served to family or at a more formal gathering. While a given meal may not be inclusive of all the courses, the order of service remains constant: hors d'oeuvre, soup, entrée with vegetables, salad, cheese, dessert and/or fruit.

No discussion of French cuisine is complete without a mention of its faithful and brilliant companion, wine. Bordeaux, Alsace and Burgundy boast some of the best vineyards in the world, the result of a happy combination of climate and soil. As much care goes into the selection and serving of wine for a meal as goes into the food itself. When choosing wines to complement a menu, there are a few guidelines that should be noted, but taste and common sense are the best guides. The first rule is to match the drinking wine with the wine used in the preparation of the dish, if any; similarly, a regional dish is best accompanied with a wine from the same region. Beyond that, it is wise to pair more delicate-flavored foods, such as fish, chicken and veal, with light-bodied and -flavored wines, primarily whites. Conversely, richer foods require wines of fuller body and flavor, generally reds. If more than one wine is being served with a meal, start with the lighter, younger wine and progress to the fuller, older one. This generally means a white followed by a red.

Savoir vivre at the table is very important. The success of a meal depends on a combination of elements, among them a well-planned menu, an attractive table setting and gracious service. French tradition demands an eye to attractive presentation. Food is arranged artistically with color and symmetry important considerations. Often an entire course is elegantly presented at table, then served in modest portions, leaving more on the serving platter for those who might desire it.

Modern trends in French cooking tend to reject the complications of certain classic dishes. Emphasis today is on fresh, high-quality ingredients, prepared simply—tasting of themselves and not disguised by overbearing sauces. Commitment to quality is balanced by interest in reducing the time spent in the preparation of food. It is in this aspect that the food processor can be invaluable to today's cook.

HOW TO CHOOSE A PROCESSOR

I thought my kitchen was well equipped until I saw a food processor. It is an appliance that nearly replaces my chopping board and knives. It will slice, chop or purée vegetables and fruits, grind meat, mix ingredients for pie crust or choux pastry, mix and knead dough for bread. It will quickly blend ingredients for mayonnaise, hollandaise, butter creams and perform countless other blending tasks. What were once complicated cooking chores, such as making quenelles or pâté, are now remarkably simple. And what's more, using fresh vegetables and fruits can now be as expedient as opening a can or frozen-food package.

Before you decide to buy a processor, however, consider whether you have the space. Most cooks find that they use their processor most frequently if it is conveniently located on the kitchen counter. Will your kitchen accommodate such an addition? Take into account, too, the number of attachments some models require. Do you have the storage space? If the answers are yes, your next step is deciding which one.

But how to choose a processor? There are many brands on the market and several of them look very much alike. All manufacturers seem to make similar claims about their products. There is also a rather wide price range.

Before choosing a processor ask to see it in action—that is, ask for a demonstration in the store. Listen to see if the motor is quiet or loud. Ask to see nuts ground or ice chopped to see how stable the machine is on the counter. Do you have to hold it down with your hands? How durable are the bowl, cover and blades? Can they be put into the dishwasher? How does the machine turn off and on? Can the cover be removed while it is operating? Be sure the processor can perform all the functions advertised by the manufacturer. Last but not least, is it manufactured by a reliable company and how do you obtain service should it be needed? Take all these factors into consideration before making a choice. A well thought out purchase will reward you with years of use and enjoyment—and hours of time saved!

HINTS ON THE USE OF A PROCESSOR

Before you operate your food processor read the instruction manual thoroughly. Require anyone in your household who is going to use the processor to read the manual. While specific operating instructions will vary with each brand, here are a few hints that apply to most processors.

Keep in mind that the action of this new appliance is almost instantaneous; practice chopping, slicing and grating a variety of foods until you feel confident in its use. When chopping foods such as onions and meat, stop the machine every two or three seconds to check for coarseness or fineness. The process is so fast that you might end up with purée if you wait a few seconds too long.

When slicing food with the slicing disc, a thicker slice may be obtained by putting pressure on the food with the plunger. With practice, you will get a feel for it. Thin and medium discs are available for varying slice thickness.

Use the plastic blade when making mayonnaise; when making hollandaise, either the plastic or steel blade may be used. If any chopping needs to be done for a hollandaise variation, use the steel blade for the entire operation.

When chopping ice or hard cheese such as Parmesan, use the steel blade. Cut large pieces to a size to fit the feed tube and add the ice or cheese after the processor is turned on. The machine may be noisy at first, but will quickly return to normal.

Check your instructions to determine the capacity of your processor bowl. Frequently a soup, sauce or batter must be blended in two or more batches. In this book the recipe will indicate when such a step is necessary.

When removing purée or batter from the processor bowl, remove bowl with blade in place from base of machine. Hold blade in place with a spatula while pouring contents into desired container. Then remove blade.

The most satisfactory results can be obtained when making pie crust if the butter and shortening are frozen. Then the fast action of the steel blade will cut the butter and shortening into pieces rather than creaming them with the flour. Turn the machine off and on frequently to check for size of butter—the pieces should be about the size of small peas.

NOTES ON USING THESE RECIPES

Freshly ground black and white peppers are used in all recipes in this book. I use a small handmill that grinds the peppercorns more coarsely than commercially ground pepper. Pepper has a tendency to lose its pungency after it is ground and allowed to remain in an open package.

Recipes do not always specify "adjust seasonings to taste." I have assumed that each cook will make adjustments of salt and pepper amounts as he or she desires.

Stocks are used extensively in the recipes and instructions for making them at home are included in Basics. Commercial stocks may be substituted, but be sure to decrease the amount of salt in the recipe.

Ovens should always be preheated to the specified temperature; most ovens require 10 to 15 minutes to come to the desired heat.

Wines to be used in these recipes are left to the cook's discretion, but should be the same or closely related to the wine one plans to serve with the dish. Generally, dry wines are best for cooking.

Cooking oils are not specified, with the exception of olive oil. Again, the cook's discretion is advised.

Hors d'Oeuvres

CHAMPIGNONS FARCIS
Stuffed Mushrooms
Serves 4

Stuffed mushrooms may be served as a first course or as an accompaniment to steaks, roast chicken or broiled fish.

12 to 16 large mushrooms
2 to 3 tablespoons melted butter
3 shallots
3 tablespoons butter
8 sprigs parsley
1/2 teaspoon tarragon
1/4 cup fine bread crumbs, see Basics
1/4 cup grated Parmesan cheese, see Basics
Salt to taste
Black pepper to taste
2 to 3 tablespoons heavy cream

Wash and remove stems from mushrooms; drain. Brush top of mushrooms with melted butter and place upside down in lightly greased shallow baking pan. Put shallots and mushroom stems in processor using steel blade; process until finely chopped. In a saucepan, sauté mushroom mixture in the 3 tablespoons butter 5 minutes. Remove from heat. Mince parsley in processor using steel blade; add to stuffing. Add remaining ingredients, using enough cream to make mixture moist. Fill caps with mixture, drizzle remaining melted butter on top. Bake in 400° oven 12 to 15 minutes. Run under broiler for a few minutes to brown top.

ESCARGOTS AU BEURRE D'AIL
Snails in Garlic Butter
Serves 4

Serve snails at your next small dinner party. They will be a sensation. Many of your friends, like mine, have never had enough courage to order them at a restaurant. To tell you a secret, they're easy to prepare.

3 cloves garlic
2 shallots or green onions
6 sprigs parsley
Dash of salt
Black pepper to taste
1/2 pound butter
24 snails and shells

Put garlic, shallots and parsley in processor using steel blade. Process until very fine. Add salt, pepper and butter; process until smooth. Drain snails, wash in water, drain again. Push about 1/2 teaspoon of butter mixture in each shell. Add the snail, small end first, pushing it into the shell. Pack with more butter. Place filled shells in snail pans or use aluminum foil to make holders for snails, butter side up. Place under broiler about 4 inches from heat for about 5 minutes. Serve with French bread to soak up butter.

BOEUF À LA TARTARE
Steak Tartar
Serves 6

This is a breeze to prepare with your food processor. It's best if you don't grind your steak too far in advance, and if you leave the meat coarsely ground.

1 pound sirloin steak
1 teaspoon salt
1/4 teaspoon black pepper
2 flat white onions
1/4 pound butter, clarified, see Basics
1 2-ounce can anchovies

Buy enough steak so that after you have trimmed away all the fat and removed the bone you have 1 pound of steak to grind. Cut meat into cubes or strips 2 to 3 inches long. Put half the meat in processor using steel blade. Process until coarsely ground and transfer to bowl. Grind remaining meat and add to bowl with salt and pepper. Cut onions into quarters; put in processor using steel blade. Process until coarsely chopped. Make a well in center of meat, add half of onions. Heat butter until it starts to turn brown, pour over onions. Mix meat, onions and butter. Shape into a mound and place on serving dish. Drain anchovies and cut each into thin strips. Weave a latticework pattern over the top. Cover remaining onions with ice water and let stand 15 minutes (this gives them a milder flavor); drain and blot dry with paper towels. Press onions around base of ball. Serve with buttered toast points or rye bread.

PÂTÉ DE FOIE DE VOLAILLE
Chicken Liver Pâté
Serves 15

A chicken liver pâté should be included in any large buffet. It can be made two days in advance. It also freezes well; allow plenty of time to thaw.

2 pounds chicken livers
1 small onion
1 clove garlic
1/2 pound butter
1 teaspoon sweet basil
Dash of black pepper
2 teaspoons anchovy paste
1 tablespoon cognac
1 tablespoon red wine
1 tablespoon sherry
Melted clarified butter, see Basics
Watercress or parsley

Make pâté the day before it is to be served. Cut livers in half; remove fat and white tissue. Cut onion into quarters, put with garlic in processor using steel blade. Process until coarsely chopped. Melt 3 tablespoons of the butter in skillet. Add livers, garlic, onion and basil; sauté about 7 minutes or until livers are barely done. Let cool, then pour all into processor using steel blade. Add remaining butter (clarified butter is for mold), pepper, anchovy paste, cognac, red wine and sherry. Process until mixture is smooth. Taste and adjust seasonings.

Brush a 3-cup mold with clarified butter, put in freezer to harden; coat again. Fill with pâté mixture. Cover with transparent wrap, refrigerate overnight. To unmold, dip in warm water, dry and set plate over mold; invert. Let pâté stand at room temperature about 1 hour before serving. If desired, decorate pâté with softened cream cheese forced through pastry tube. Decorate plate with watercress or parsley. Serve with toast points.

THON À LA MIROMESNIL
Tuna Fish Cream
Serves 6

1/2 pound cooked fresh or canned tuna
1/4 cup heavy cream
1 tablespoon mayonnaise
1 teaspoon fresh lemon juice
Dash of cayenne pepper
1/2 clove garlic
Salt to taste
1 tablespoon sliced black olives

If using fresh tuna, remove skin and bone. If using canned tuna, drain. Put tuna, cream, mayonnaise, lemon juice, pepper and garlic in processor using steel blade. Process until smooth. (Mixture will be very thick.) Add salt. Butter a 1-cup mold; add tuna mixture and chill overnight. Dip mold into hot water, dry and turn upside down on serving tray. Decorate with black olive slices. Serve with fingers of thin toast.

CHOUX AU CRABE
Crab-Filled Puffs
Serves 8

Miniature puffs make excellent finger food. The puffs may be made several days in advance, stored in an airtight container and filled the day served. If they have lost some of their crispness, simply reheat in a slow oven (300°) for 15 to 20 minutes.

Pâté à Choux (Cream Puff Pastry)
1 cup water
6 tablespoons butter
1/8 teaspoon salt
1 cup flour
3 large eggs
1 additional egg
1/2 teaspoon water

Put water, butter and salt in heavy saucepan. Bring mixture to boil; boil until butter melts. Remove from heat, add flour all at once and beat vigorously with wooden spoon to blend in flour. Return to moderate heat; stir and cook for several minutes. Pastry will clean itself off sides and bottom of pan. Continue cooking and beating 2 to 3 minutes longer, thus evaporating excess moisture. Remove from heat, spoon into processor using steel blade. With processor on, add 3 eggs through feed tube 1 at a time. Be sure each egg is mixed in thoroughly before adding the next. Pastry should be stiff enough to hold its shape when lifted in a spoon. Use immediately or keep warm over hot water.

For hors d'oeuvre-size puffs, spoon paste into pastry bag using a 1/2-inch round tube opening. Squeeze the pastry onto a buttered baking sheet, making mounds about the size of walnuts. Combine the additional egg with the water; dip a pastry brush into egg and slightly flatten each puff using side of brush. (Avoid dripping egg down puff onto baking sheet.) Bake in 400° oven 30 to 40 minutes or until golden brown and crisp. Remove from oven, slice off top, remove soft centers. Puffs may be used immediately or will keep 1 to 2 days in an airtight container. They may also be frozen. If puffs are frozen they should be heated in 400° oven 5 to 7 minutes to make crisp again. Makes 24 to 30 puffs.

Fondue de Crabe (Crab Meat Filling)
2 shallots or 3 green onions
4 tablespoons butter
1/2 pound fresh crab meat
1/3 cup dry white wine
1/8 teaspoon salt
Black pepper to taste
2 tablespoons flour
1 cup milk or fish stock, see Basics
Salt to taste
1 egg yolk
1/4 cup grated Parmesan cheese, see Basics

Put shallots or white part of onions in processor using steel blade. Process until finely chopped. Melt 2 tablespoons butter in saucepan. Add onions and sauté for 5 minutes. Flake crab meat and remove the tissuelike membrane. Add crab meat and wine to onion mixture. Cover and simmer 1 minute. Uncover, increase heat and boil rapidly until all liquid has evaporated. Season with salt and pepper. Set aside and make sauce.

In saucepan, melt remaining 2 tablespoons butter, add flour, stir and cook 2 minutes. Gradually add milk or stock. Bring mixture to boil, stirring constantly. Boil 1 minute. Add salt. Beat egg yolk, add 6 tablespoons of hot sauce, stir together. Add all of egg mixture to sauce, stirring constantly. Cook 1 minute longer. Stir in crab meat and cheese. Use immediately to fill puff shells or press plastic wrap on top of sauce to prevent a film from forming. Filling may be made hours in advance, cooled and refrigerated. Then after puffs are filled, heat in 375° oven 10 to 12 minutes. Makes about 1-1/2 cups filling.

Note The crab filling is also excellent as a filling for crêpes. Will fill 6 to 8 6-inch crêpes.

PÂTÉ BRISÉE FINE
Pastry Shell
Makes 1 8-inch pastry shell

1 cup flour
1/8 teaspoon salt
3 tablespoons butter, frozen
2 tablespoons shortening, frozen
2 to 3 tablespoons ice water

Place flour and salt in processor using steel blade. Cut butter into 1-inch pieces, add along with shortening. Process until butter is cut into flour (about 10 seconds). With processor on, gradually add water through feed tube until mixture forms a ball (you may not need all the water). Watch constantly, do not overmix. Wrap in wax paper and chill 2 hours before using. (If short of time, chill at least 30 minutes.) Chilling firms butter and relaxes gluten in flour. On a floured board, roll dough into circle 2 inches larger than an 8-inch quiche pan or pie plate. Fit dough into pan, trim and crimp edges. Add filling and bake according to filling recipe directions.

For a more crisp and brown bottom crust prebake pastry. Butter a large sheet of lightweight aluminum foil and fit buttered side down in pastry. Fill with dried beans and bake in 450° oven 7 to 8 minutes. Remove from oven, check sides and if necessary repair with pastry trimmings. Return to oven and bake 5 minutes longer. Crust will be just beginning to brown. Remove beans and foil; let cool. Add filling and bake as directed in recipe.

QUICHE JAMBON
Ham and Onion Pie
Serves 8

1 8-inch pastry shell (Pâté Brisée Fine), preceding
1/2 cup diced cooked ham
1/2 clove garlic
1/2 medium onion
1 tablespoon oil
3 ounces Swiss cheese
2 eggs
1 cup half-and-half cream
Dash of nutmeg
1/4 teaspoon salt
Dash of black pepper

Prepare pastry as directed in recipe. Sprinkle ham over bottom of pastry. Put garlic in processor using steel blade. Process until very fine. Cut onion in half, put in processor with finely chopped garlic, process until coarsely chopped. Cook onion and garlic in oil over low heat until tender (about 5 minutes). Sprinkle onion over ham. Cut cheese into thin strips, sprinkle over onion. Put eggs in processor using steel blade. Add remaining ingredients and process until blended. Pour over ham and cheese. Bake in 350° oven 20 to 25 minutes or until set. Test for doneness by inserting knife in center. It should come out clean. Serve hot.

Note This recipe will also serve 4 for lunch or supper.

QUICHE LORRAINE
Bacon and Onion Pie
Serves 8

A quiche may be sliced very thin and served as an hors d'oeuvre, cut into larger slices and served as main entrée for lunch, or included in a brunch, buffet or midnight supper.

1 8-inch pastry shell (Pâté Brisée Fine), preceding
8 slices bacon
1/2 clove garlic
1/2 medium onion
2 eggs
1 cup half-and-half cream
Dash of nutmeg
1/4 teaspoon salt
Dash of black pepper
1/4 cup grated Parmesan cheese, see Basics

Prepare pastry shell as directed in recipe. Cut bacon into pieces about 1/4 inch wide; brown lightly in skillet. Drain, reserving fat, and sprinkle bacon on bottom of pastry shell. Put garlic in processor using steel blade. Process until very fine. Cut onion in half, put in processor with finely chopped garlic, process until coarsely chopped. Cook onion and garlic in 1 tablespoon of the bacon fat until tender. Sprinkle onion over bacon. Put eggs in processor using steel blade. Add remaining ingredients and process until blended; pour over bacon. Bake in 350° oven 20 to 25 minutes or until barely set in center. Test for doneness by inserting knife in center. It should come out clean. Serve while hot.

Note This recipe will also serve 4 for lunch or supper.

Soups

Potages

SOUPE À L'OIGNON
Onion Soup
Serves 6

4 medium onions
4 tablespoons butter
1/4 teaspoon sugar
1 tablespoon flour
6 cups beef stock, see Basics
1 teaspoon salt
Black pepper to taste
6 thick slices French bread
1/2 cup grated Parmesan cheese, see Basics

Cut onions in half. Slice onions in processor using slicing disc. In heavy saucepan, melt 3 tablespoons of the butter; add onions, sprinkle with sugar and cook on medium heat. Stir frequently and cook until onions are brown. (This will take 15 or 20 minutes.) Add flour; blend in and cook 2 minutes longer. Gradually add stock while stirring constantly. Season with salt and pepper. Bring mixture to boil, reduce heat and simmer uncovered for 30 minutes.

Meanwhile place bread on baking sheet. Bake in 300° oven about 20 minutes or until thoroughly dry and light brown. Melt remaining 1 tablespoon butter and lightly brush each side of bread with melted butter.

When ready to serve, spoon soup into soup tureen or 6 individual pottery soup bowls. Place toast on top of soup, sprinkle with cheese and place under heated broiler long enough to melt cheese.

POTAGE POMMES DE TERRE
Potato Soup
Serves 8

8 sprigs parsley
2 medium potatoes, peeled
2 medium onions
3 leeks, if available
4 cups chicken stock, see Basics
4 cups water
1 tablespoon salt
1/8 teaspoon white pepper
3 tablespoons butter

Put parsley in processor using steel blade. Process until minced; remove. Slice potatoes, onions and leeks in processor using slicing disc. In large saucepan combine all ingredients except butter; simmer 40 minutes. Use a large slotted spoon and dip out about three quarters of the potatoes and onions. Put in processor using steel blade. Process a few seconds until potatoes are partly puréed but still lumpy. Return potato mixture to saucepan; add butter. Serve hot.

Vichyssoise (Cold Potato Soup) Put about 4 cups potato soup in processor using steel blade. Process until smooth. Repeat with remaining soup. Add cream to obtain desired consistency. Chill for several hours. Taste for seasoning (cold food requires more salt).

Potage au Cresson Froid (Cold Watercress Soup) Add 1 cup watercress leaves and stems to potato soup the last 5 minutes of simmering. Purée, chill and season as for Vichyssoise.

POTAGE À LA LAITUE
Lettuce Soup
Serves 4

Lettuce soup is especially attractive and has a delicate flavor. It is a light soup and can be served with a large meal.

1 firm head iceberg lettuce (6 to 8 inches in diameter)
2 tablespoons butter
2 tablespoons uncooked rice
4 cups chicken stock, see Basics
1/2 teaspoon salt
1/8 teaspoon white pepper

Remove any wilted outer leaves of the lettuce and discard. Rinse head under cold water, cut into quarters and remove core. Slice lettuce in processor using slicing disc. Melt butter in heavy saucepan over medium heat. Add lettuce and toss with spoon to coat evenly with butter. Reduce heat, cook 5 minutes, stirring frequently. Add rice, chicken stock, salt and pepper. Simmer 10 to 15 minutes or until rice is barely tender. Pour into heated tureen or individual soup bowls.

POTAGE CAROTTES
Carrot Soup
Serves 4

1/2 pound carrots
1 onion
6 tablespoons butter
3 tablespoons uncooked rice
4 cups chicken stock, see Basics
1 sprig thyme or dash of dry thyme
1/2 teaspoon salt
1/8 teaspoon black pepper

Slice carrots and onion in processor using slicing disc. Melt 4 tablespoons of the butter in saucepan; add carrots and onion; cover and simmer 5 minutes. Add remaining ingredients; simmer 30 minutes. Discard sprig of thyme if used. In processor using steel blade process soup in two batches till smooth. Return all to saucepan; heat and add remaining 2 tablespoons of butter. If soup is too thick, add small amount of water.

POTAGE D'ÉPINARDS
Spinach Soup
Serves 6

1/4 pound butter
3 leeks or green onions
2 onions
1 carrot
2 teaspoons salt
1 teaspoon sugar
Black pepper to taste
3 medium potatoes, peeled and quartered
5 cups chicken stock (see Basics) or water
1/2 pound fresh spinach
1/4 cup heavy cream
2 egg yolks
6 sprigs parsley

Melt butter in large saucepan. Slice leeks (using white part), onions and carrot in processor using slicing disc; add to butter. Cover and simmer 20 minutes. Add salt, sugar, pepper, potatoes and stock; cover and simmer 1 hour. Wash spinach and remove stems and tough veins; add to soup for last 5 minutes cooking time. Using steel blade, process soup in three batches until smooth. Pour all back into saucepan. When ready to serve, combine cream and yolks, stir in small amount of soup mixture, then pour all back into saucepan. Heat and stir, do not boil. Chop parsley in processor using steel blade. Serve soup topped with parsley.

POTAGE DE LÉGUMES
Bean Soup
Serves 4

1/2 pound small white dried beans (1-1/4 cups)
3 cups water
2 cups chicken stock, see Basics
1 medium onion
1 carrot
1 stalk celery
1 bay leaf
1 sprig parsley
Pinch thyme
1 teaspoon salt
1 cup milk
4 tablespoons butter
1/2 cup croûtons

Put beans in bowl; cover with water and soak overnight. Put beans and liquid in large saucepan; add chicken stock. Cut onion into quarters and carrot into 2-inch pieces; put into processor using steel blade; process until coarsely chopped. Add to beans with celery, bay leaf, parsley, thyme and salt. Cover and simmer 2 hours or until beans are very tender. Discard celery, bay leaf and parsley. Using steel blade process soup in three batches until smooth. Pour all back into saucepan; add milk and butter. Bring to boiling point, do not boil. Serve hot with croûtons on top.

CRÈME DE POIS
Cream of Pea Soup
Serves 4

1 medium onion
1 small carrot
4 tablespoons butter
3 to 4 lettuce leaves
2 cups fresh or frozen green peas
1 slice boiled or baked ham or hambone
3 cups water
1-1/2 teaspoons salt
1/8 teaspoon thyme
1/2 teaspoon tarragon
1/2 cup whipped cream

Cut onion into quarters and carrot into 2-inch lengths. Put both in processor using steel blade and process until coarsely chopped. Heat butter in heavy saucepan; add onion-carrot mixture and lettuce; cook 5 to 8 minutes or until onion is transparent. Add peas, ham, water, salt, thyme and tarragon. Bring ingredients to boil, reduce to simmer and simmer 40 minutes. Remove ham and discard. Purée soup in processor using steel blade. Return to saucepan and if too thick, thin with water or milk.

At serving time, heat soup to simmer, stirring constantly. Spoon into bowls. Add a dollop of whipped cream.

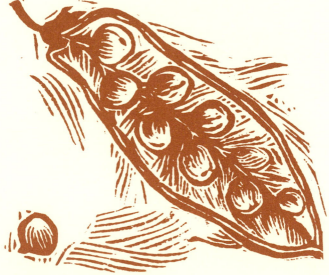

SAUMON BISQUE
Chilled Salmon Bisque
Serves 4

1/2 clove garlic
1 small onion
1/2 green pepper
1 carrot
1 tablespoon butter
1 7-1/2-ounce can salmon
1-1/2 cups milk
1/2 teaspoon dill weed
1/8 teaspoon cayenne pepper
1/8 teaspoon nutmeg
1/8 teaspoon white pepper
1 teaspoon salt
1/2 cup heavy cream
2 sprigs parsley

Put garlic in processor using steel blade, process until minced. Cut onion into quarters; cut pepper into 4 parts; cut carrot into 2-inch lengths; put all into processor with garlic. Process until coarsely chopped. Melt butter in heavy saucepan, add vegetables. Sauté until tender (about 6 to 10 minutes). Return sautéed vegetables to processor, again using steel blade. Add undrained salmon, milk, seasonings and cream. Process until mixture is smooth. Chill before serving. Serve in soup tureen or individual soup bowls. Chop parsley in processor using steel blade; sprinkle over top of each serving.

Seafood
Fruits de Mer

COQUILLES ST. JACQUES PARISIENNE
Sea Scallops in White Wine Sauce
Serves 4

Scallops are very tender and have a delicate taste. When overcooked they taste like cotton, so take care in their preparation.

1-1/2 pounds sea scallops
1-1/2 cups dry white wine
1/2 teaspoon salt
1/4 teaspoon white pepper
6 tablespoons butter
2 shallots
1/4 pound mushrooms
1/4 cup flour
1 cup milk
1/2 cup grated Parmesan cheese, see Basics
2 to 3 tablespoons fine bread crumbs, see Basics

Wash scallops and keep in water until ready to cook. In saucepan combine scallops, wine, salt and pepper; bring to boil and simmer for 5 minutes.

Drain scallops, reserving cooking liquid, and set aside. If scallops are large, cut in half. Measure cooking liquid and if necessary boil rapidly to reduce to 1 cup. Melt 4 tablespoons of the butter in a separate saucepan. Put shallots in processor using steel blade; process until finely chopped. Add to butter and cook on low heat 5 minutes. Remove stems from mushrooms; slice caps in processor using slicing disc. Slice stems. Add both to shallots and cook 1 minute longer. Add flour and stir in. Continue to stir and gradually add cooking liquid; add milk. Stir constantly and cook 2 or 3 minutes longer until slightly thickened. Remove from heat; add scallops and cheese. Taste; if necessary, add more salt. Fill buttered shells or individual casseroles. Sprinkle with bread crumbs. Dot with remaining butter. Place under broiler until tops are brown.

Note Shrimp, shelled and deveined, may be used in place of scallops. Recipe will also serve 6 as a first course.

COQUILLES ST. JACQUES NANTAISE
Scallops in Parsley Butter
Serves 4

1-1/2 pounds sea scallops
Salt
Black pepper
6 shallots
1/4 pound butter
4 sprigs parsley
1/2 cup fine bread crumbs, see Basics

Wash scallops and keep in water until ready to cook. Dry, cut in half, sprinkle with salt and pepper; put into six buttered shells or individual casseroles. Put shallots in processor using steel blade, process until finely chopped. Cook in 2 tablespoons butter 5 to 7 minutes or until soft; sprinkle over scallops. Melt remaining butter, drizzle over all. Put parsley in processor using steel blade; process until finely chopped. Combine parsley and crumbs, sprinkle on top. Put in 375° oven and cook 12 to 15 minutes or until scallops are tender when pierced with a fork. Serve at once.

Note Recipe will also serve 6 as a first course.

ENTRÉE CRÊPES
Makes 16 to 18 6-inch crêpes

1 cup milk
2 eggs
1 cup flour
Dash of salt
2 tablespoons melted butter

In order listed, put ingredients in processor using steel blade. Process until thoroughly blended. Pour batter into bowl and refrigerate 2 hours. Heat a cast-iron crêpe pan (6 or 7 inches in diameter) over moderately high heat until a drop of water dances on bottom. Moisten a paper napkin with oil and rub inside of skillet. Pour 2 or 3 tablespoons batter into pan. Tilt pan to spread batter evenly. When brown on one side, loosen edge with blunt knife, turn and cook other side 1 or 2 seconds. Turn out on rack and let cool. Repeat with remaining batter, rubbing pan with oiled napkin after cooking each crêpe.

CRÊPES AUX CRUSTACÉS
Seafood Crêpes
Serves 6

Sauce Mornay
2 tablespoons butter
2 tablespoons cornstarch
1-1/2 cups half-and-half cream
1/4 teaspoon salt
Dash of black pepper
1/4 pound Swiss cheese

1/2 medium onion
2 tablespoons butter
1/4 pound mushrooms
1-1/2 cups cooked seafood (shrimp, crab
    meat or lobster)
Salt to taste
Black pepper to taste
1/4 cup white vermouth
12 to 14 Entrée Crêpes, preceding

Melt butter; add cornstarch, stir and add cream. Cook on medium heat, stirring constantly until thick. Add salt and pepper. With shredding disc in processor, grate cheese. Add half of cheese to sauce, reserving remaining half.

Cut onion in half; put in processor using steel blade. Process until finely chopped. Melt butter in saucepan; add onion and sauté 5 minutes. Put mushrooms in processor using steel blade and process until coarsely chopped. Add mushrooms and remaining ingredients except crêpes to onion mixture. Boil rapidly until liquid is almost entirely evaporated. Add half of Sauce Mornay to seafood mixture. Place big spoonful of filling on lower third of each crêpe; roll. Arrange crêpes close together in lightly buttered baking dish. Spoon rest of sauce over top and sprinkle remaining Swiss cheese over all. Bake in 425° oven 15 to 20 minutes or until thoroughly heated.

SOLE BONNE FEMME
Sole with Mushrooms and White Wine Sauce
Serves 6

Sole Bonne Femme is easy to prepare, especially when the processor does the slicing and chopping. The total cooking time is 20 minutes or less depending on the thickness of the fish.

8 mushrooms
4 shallots
3 sprigs parsley
1 pound sole fillets
Salt
Black pepper
6 tablespoons dry white wine
6 tablespoons water
2 egg yolks
2 tablespoons butter

Butter an ovenproof dish large enough to hold fillets in single layer. Remove stems from mushrooms; trim off tough bottoms. Slice caps in processor using slicing disc; sprinkle in dish. Put mushroom stems, shallots and parsley in processor using steel blade; process until coarsely chopped; spread over mushrooms. Arrange fillets on top. Sprinkle with salt and pepper; add wine and water; bring to boil; cover with buttered wax paper. Put in 325° oven and cook 20 minutes. Baste after 10 minutes, lifting paper and spooning liquid over fish. At end of cooking time, check to see that fish flakes easily. Discard paper. Tilt dish and spoon off liquid. Beat egg yolks and gradually add hot cooking liquid. Add butter and stir until it melts. Pour sauce over fish. Brown under broiler.

FILETS DE SOLE FARCIS
Stuffed Fillets of Sole
Serves 8

1/2 pound mushrooms
4 tablespoons butter
Salt to taste
Black pepper to taste
Dash of sugar
1/2 cup dry white wine
8 fillets of sole
2 tablespoons flour
1/2 cup half-and-half cream
Dash of nutmeg

Trim tough bottoms from mushroom stems; put mushrooms in processor using steel blade; process until coarsely chopped. Melt 2 tablespoons of the butter in saucepan, add mushrooms, sauté 2 minutes. Season with salt, pepper and sugar. Butter an oval skillet or pan; add wine. Lay four fillets in wine, cover with mushrooms; top with remaining fillets. Cut wax paper to fit pan, butter one side, fit buttered side down over fillets. Bring to a boil; boil 5 minutes.

While fish cooks make sauce. Melt remaining 2 tablespoons butter in saucepan, add flour and cook 3 minutes. Add cream and nutmeg. Cook, stirring constantly till thickened. Remove cooked fillets to hot overproof platter. Strain liquid into sauce. Stir and cook 3 minutes longer. Spoon over fillets. Brown under broiler. To serve, cut across middle of each fillet.

POISSON AU FOUR
Baked Fish
Serves 4

2 medium onions
4 lemons
4 trout or perch (8 to 10 ounces each), cleaned,
    heads and tails intact
Salt
Black pepper
6 tablespoons butter
1/2 cup dry white wine

Cut onions in half; slice in processor using slicing disc. Peel lemons, cutting deep enough to remove white pith. Using processor with slicing disc, slice lemons. Check fish to make sure they are well cleaned. Leave heads on and sprinkle inside and out with salt and pepper. Generously butter the bottom of a dish large enough to hold fish in one layer. Spread half the sliced onions in dish; add a quarter of the sliced lemons. Arrange fish on top of this. Cover with remaining onion and lemon. Dot with butter. Bake in 375° oven about 30 minutes or until fish is tender. Check with fork to see if meat is tender. As fish cooks, baste several times with a little wine or water to keep it moist. Serve from baking dish.

TRUITE EN PAPILLOTE
Trout in Paper Case
Serves 4

Cook and serve each person his or her own trout in its own paper case. The preparation time is short with the processor doing the chopping. Most any lean fish can be cooked in a paper case.

Duxelles (Mushroom Mixture)
1 shallot
1/4 pound mushrooms
2 tablespoons butter
3 sprigs parsley
Salt to taste
Black pepper to taste

4 speckled trout, cleaned, head and tails intact
2 to 3 tablespoons butter
Salt
Black pepper
Lemon wedges

Chop shallot very fine in processor using steel blade. Add mushrooms and process until finely chopped. In heavy saucepan, melt butter, add mushroom mixture. Cook on medium-high heat 3 to 5 minutes, stirring until all moisture has evaporated. Remove from heat. Chop parsley in processor using steel blade. Add parsley to mushrooms, season to taste with salt and pepper.

Wash fish; dry thoroughly. Cut four ovals of baking parchment or brown wrapping paper large enough to enclose each fish. Spread the center of each oval generously with butter, place the fish on top and sprinkle with salt and pepper, including the stomach cavity. Spread the duxelles on top. Fold the paper over the fish, fold the edges over twice. Moisten edges with beaten egg if regular brown paper is used. Set the packages on a baking sheet and bake in 350° oven for 15 to 18 minutes. Let each person open his own package. Wedge of lemon may be served on side.

Note To prepare in advance, cool the duxelles before spreading on fish. Prepare packages and refrigerate until ready to bake. May be prepared 3 to 4 hours in advance.

LE LOUP EN CROÛTE
Whole Striped Bass in Crust
Serves 4 to 6

Le Loup en Croûte is a work of art, a thing of beauty. A whole striped bass (head and tail intact) is enclosed in a brioche dough and decorated to look like a fish.

2 recipes Pâté à Brioche dough, page 89
1 2-1/2 pound striped bass, cleaned and scaled
       with head on
Salt
Black pepper
8 sprigs parsley
1 egg
1 teaspoon water
Lemon wedges

Prepare yeast dough one recipe at a time as directed in recipe; let rise till tripled. While dough is rising, wash and dry fish, salt and pepper inside, put parsley sprigs in cavity. Using wax paper, cut a silhouette of the fish. Punch down one recipe of dough, turn out on lightly floured cloth or board. Roll into a rectangle long enough to cut form of fish. Using wax paper fish pattern, cut dough out about 1/2 inch larger all around. Place on a lightly greased baking sheet. Lay fish on dough. Roll out second recipe of dough. Use pattern and cut about 1 inch larger. Place on top of fish; press the two layers of dough together all around and tuck under fish. Beat egg; add water to make an egg glaze. Brush fish with egg glaze. Roll out scraps of dough; form mouth, eye and back fin. Attach to fish and brush again with egg glaze. Using a metal decorating tube or small knife, cut snips in surface of dough to simulate scales. Bake immediately before dough has a chance to rise, so it will remain thin and crusty. Bake in 400° oven 45 minutes or until crust is brown and slightly puffed. Serve immediately with lemon wedges. To serve, cut around outside edge of crust and lift top crust off. Peel skin off top of fish, serve top fillet. Remove bone and serve bottom fillet. Cut a strip of the top crust for each serving. (The bottom crust will be soggy and is not served.)

FILETS DE FLET FARCIS
Stuffed Flounder with Shrimp Sauce
Serves 4

Flounder fillets spread with fish mousse, rolled and poached in wine, hold their shape well. Then for a final touch they are topped with Shrimp Sauce. A taste treat.

1/2 pound halibut or trout fillets
1 shallot
1/4 clove garlic
3/4 teaspoon salt
1/4 teaspoon white pepper
2 egg whites
1/3 cup half-and-half cream
4 medium flounder fillets
Additional salt
1/2 cup dry white wine
1/2 cup water
1 bay leaf
3 peppercorns

Dry halibut or trout with paper towel, remove skin if it has not been already removed. Cut fish into pieces 2 or 3 inches long; put in processor using steel blade. Cut shallot in half; add along with garlic, 3/4 teaspoon salt and pepper. Process until fish is puréed. Continue processing and add egg whites one at a time. With processor still on add cream, 1 tablespoon at a time, until mixture easily falls from a spoon. (You may not need all of cream.) Lay flounder on wax paper, remove skin, sprinkle both sides with salt. Spread each piece with mousse and roll up like a jelly roll; fasten with toothpick. Place rolls in lightly greased baking dish. (They may be very close together.) Add wine, water, bay leaf and peppercorns. Cover with buttered wax paper. Bake in 325° oven 15 to 20 minutes or until fish flakes easily. Remove from oven, transfer rolls to warm serving dish; remove toothpicks. Use liquid to make Shrimp Sauce.

Crevettes Bercy (Shrimp Sauce)
1 shallot
2 tablespoons butter
2 tablespoons flour
3/4 cup poaching liquid
1 tablespoon tomato paste
1/2 cup half-and-half cream
1/4 to 1/2 pound small cooked shrimp

Cut shallot in half; put in processor using steel blade. Process until finely chopped. Heat butter in saucepan; add shallot and cook on medium heat 5 minutes. Stir in flour. Stir constantly and gradually add poaching liquid. Add tomato paste and continue cooking and stirring until thick. Add cream and shrimp; heat thoroughly. Spoon sauce over rolls; reheat in 325° oven 10 minutes. Makes about 1-1/2 cups sauce.

SOUFFLÉ ROULÉ FARCI AUX CRABES
Soufflé Roll with Crab Meat Filling
Serves 6

4 tablespoons butter
1/4 cup flour
1-1/2 cups milk
4 egg yolks
1/2 teaspoon salt
1 ounce cheddar cheese
5 egg whites
1/8 teaspoon cream of tartar

Filling
1/2 medium onion
4 tablespoons butter
1/2 pound fresh or frozen crab meat or
   1 7-1/2-ounce can crab meat
1/2 cup dry white wine
2 tablespoons flour
1/2 cup fish stock, see Basics
1/2 cup water
2 teaspoons fresh lemon juice
Salt to taste
Black pepper to taste

Melt butter in saucepan; add flour, stir and cook about 2 minutes; add milk and cook, stirring constantly until thick. Beat egg yolks, stir in small amount of hot sauce; then add yolk mixture to remaining sauce. Stir for about 2 minutes, add salt. Grate cheese in processor using grating disc. Beat egg whites until frothy, add cream of tartar and continue beating until whites form stiff peaks; fold a small amount of whites into sauce; then fold in remaining whites and cheese.

Line bottom and sides of a 9 by 13 by 1-inch baking pan (jelly roll pan) with foil. Generously butter foil, sprinkle with flour, then turn upside down to remove excess flour. Gently pour soufflé mixture into prepared pan, spread evenly and bake in 375° oven 18 to 20 minutes or until done.

While soufflé cooks prepare filling. Cut onion in half; put in processor using steel blade. Process until coarsely chopped. Cook onion in 2 tablespoons of the butter about 5 minutes or until onion is tender. Flake crab meat and remove the tissue-like membrane; add crab meat to onion. Add 1/4 cup of the wine and cook on medium heat until wine is reduced to 1 teaspoon. Remove from heat while making sauce.

Melt remaining 2 tablespoons butter in saucepan. Add flour, stir in and cook 2 minutes. Add fish stock, water and remaining wine. Cook on medium heat, stirring constantly, until thick. Add lemon juice, season with salt and pepper. Reheat crab meat and add 6 tablespoons of sauce.

When soufflé is cooked, dip a dishtowel in warm water, wring out completely and spread on a flat surface. Immediately invert cooked soufflé over the towel. Carefully pull off foil. Spread crab meat filling evenly over top. Roll up from one of the long sides; slice crosswise into 1-1/2-inch slices. If not served immediately, loosely cover with foil and place in warm oven. Serve pinwheels with remaining sauce.

VOL-AU-VENT
Large Pastry Shell with Seafood Filling
Serves 4

This is an elegant dish for a luncheon or buffet. The shell must be made in advance since it does take a considerable amount of time. Make the seafood filling the day of serving.

Pâté Feuilletée (Puff Pastry)
2 cups flour
1/4 teaspoon salt
1/2 pound butter
1 teaspoon fresh lemon juice
About 2/3 cup ice water
Additional flour
1 egg

Put flour and salt into processor using steel blade. Cut 1 tablespoon of butter into three pieces; add. Turn processor on for a few seconds to cut butter into flour. Combine lemon juice and water. With processor on add lemon-water mixture steadily just until flour is moist and mixture forms a ball; turn off processor. Remove dough and wrap in plastic wrap or put in plastic bag; chill 15 minutes.

Lightly dust the remaining butter, using about 2 teaspoons flour. Put butter between two sheets wax paper; pound with rolling pin to flatten. Fold butter, again place between wax paper and continue pounding and folding (use more flour if butter becomes sticky) until pliable but not sticky. Shape butter into a 5-inch square and flour lightly.

Roll out dough on floured formica or marble counter to a 12-inch square, leaving a hump in the center. To do this, start rolling the dough about 2 inches from the center and roll toward edge; do not roll all the way across the square. Set the square of butter in the center and fold the dough around it like an envelope. Wrap in plastic and chill 15 minutes.

Put the dough back on floured work surface, flap side up; bring rolling pin down on dough three to four times to flatten slightly. Roll it out to a rectangle 5 to 6 inches wide and 14 to 15 inches long. Fold the top third of dough down over the center third; then fold up the bottom third of dough (like a letter). Seal the edges with the rolling pin and give the dough a quarter turn to bring open ends to top and bottom. Repeat, rolling dough into 5 by 14-inch rectangle, folding like a letter, and sealing open ends. Keep a record of these "turns" by marking the dough lightly with the appropriate number of fingerprints (two prints at this point). Wrap dough in plastic and chill 15 minutes.

Repeat the rolling and folding process, giving the dough six turns all together, with a 15-minute rest in the refrigerator between every two turns. Chill 15 minutes before using.

Pastry may be kept, tightly wrapped, in the refrigerator for up to a week, or up to 3 months in the freezer.

(Continued on Next Page)

Forming Vol-au-Vent

Roll out the puff pastry to a 7 by 14-inch rectangle and cut into two 6-inch rounds, using a plate or lid as a guide. Turn over one round, set it on a dampened baking sheet. (Damp surface makes pastry stick to sheet, giving it a grip so that it can rise in the oven.) Cut a 1-inch ring from the remaining circle, using a 4-inch round plate or lid as guide. (Refrigerate 4-inch circle.) Brush outer 1-inch edge of uncut circle with water. Place ring on moistened edge of circle. Scallop and seal the two layers of dough together by using the back of a small knife and pressing slanting parallel lines 1/8 inch deep and about 1 inch apart all around the circumference. Press down top of circle with your fingers as you prepare edge. Beat the egg and brush ring and circle with egg glaze. (Do not let glaze run down side to baking sheet; this would prevent pastry from rising.) With a small knife cut lines 1/8 inch deep in top of ring, pointing knife to the center so the marks will look like the spokes of a wheel. Lines should be about 1-1/2 inches apart at the outside edge. Cut a line 1/8 inch deep in the pastry circle where the inner edge of ring meets it. Make shallow lines in the pastry circle just through the glaze with the point of a knife, about 1 inch apart—first going right to left and then top to bottom. Plunge point of knife through the ring and

bottom circle at 4 or 5 places. (This holds the puff layers together and helps pastry rise evenly.) Prick with knife in center area three times. Cover pastry shell lightly and chill in refrigerator 1 hour.

To prepare cover, remove chilled 4-inch circle from refrigerator. Roll into a larger circle and cut into a 6-inch round. Scallop edge in spoke fashion with the back of knife at 3/4-inch intervals. Put on baking sheet with pastry shell or put on separate baking sheet. Prick circle with tines of fork going down through pastry. Prick close together. (Pricking discourages dough from rising.) Cover and chill in refrigerator 1 hour before baking.

Bake both shell and cover in 425° oven 25 to 30 minutes or until puffed and browned. As soon as you remove Vol-au-Vent shell from oven, cut around the inside edge of the ring and remove the circle of dough you marked in the bottom circle. (Set aside for another use.) Carefully scrape unbaked pastry from bottom of shell using the tines of a fork. Be careful not to pierce sides or bottom of crust. Remove cover to cooling rack. Return shell to 350° oven for 10 to 15 minutes to dry out more thoroughly. Shell and cover may be kept at room temperature 3 to 4 days in an airtight container. Or shell and cover may be frozen. Wrap airtight and freeze; will keep several weeks.

Fruits de Mer (Seafood Filling)
1 tablespoon butter
3/4 pound fresh or canned oysters with liquor
1/2 pound mushrooms
Juice of 1/2 lemon
1/8 teaspoon salt
Dash of black pepper
1/2 pound cooked shrimp

Sauce Parisienne (White Sauce with Egg Yolks)
3 tablespoons butter
3 tablespoons flour
2 cups fish stock, see Basics
3/4 cup combined liquid from oysters and
    mushrooms, above
2 egg yolks
1/4 cup heavy cream
1/8 teaspoon salt

In saucepan melt butter, add oysters and their liquor and cook 1 to 2 minutes until the edges curl. Let cool; drain and reserve liquid. Remove stems from mushrooms; slice caps in processor using slicing disc (reserve stems for another use). Put sliced mushroom caps in a pan with lemon juice, salt and pepper. Add water to a depth of 1/4 inch; cover pan and cook 4 to 5 minutes. Drain and reserve liquid. Combine liquid from mushrooms with liquid from oysters; measure. If amount of combined liquids exceeds 3/4 cup, place in saucepan and boil down to 3/4 cup. If amount is less, add water to make 3/4 cup. Set aside for use in sauce. Peel and devein shrimp; set aside.

To make sauce, melt butter in saucepan, add flour, stir and cook for 2 minutes. Gradually add fish stock and oyster-mushroom liquid. Bring mixture to a boil, stirring constantly. Boil 1 minute. Combine egg yolks and cream in a bowl; stir in a little of the hot sauce; then add egg mixture to sauce, stirring constantly. Heat a few minutes longer. Do not let boil. Add salt, oysters, mushrooms and shrimp. Use immediately to fill Vol-au-Vent or keep hot up to 20 minutes in a water bath.

When ready to serve, reheat pastry shell and cover by setting on a lightly buttered baking sheet and baking in 325° oven for 10 to 15 minutes. If frozen, heat in 325° oven 15 to 20 minutes. Set heated shell on platter, add filling and put cover on at a slant. Cut out portion of shell, put on plate. Add spoonful of seafood filling. If desired cut and serve part of cover.

QUENELLES DE POISSON I
Fish Dumplings with Oysters and White Wine Sauce
Serves 6

Fish quenelles are light and delicate. They may be served as a first course at a formal dinner or as the main entrée for lunch or supper. I like to make an extra large quantity and freeze some for later use.

1/2 pound flounder, haddock or sole fillets
2 eggs
3 egg whites
1/4 teaspoon salt
Dash of white pepper
4 cups fish stock, see Basics
2 tablespoons melted butter
1 pint oysters

Dry fillets on paper towels, cut into 2-inch lengths. Put fish into processor using steel blade. Process until ground. With processor on add eggs through feed tube, one at a time. Add egg whites, one at a time. Add salt and pepper. Put mixture into a small bowl. Heat stock in skillet or saucepan to simmer. (Liquid should be about 2-1/2 inches deep.) If stock is not salted add 1/2 teaspoon salt. Use two teaspoons to shape quenelles. Dip first teaspoon in cold water, then dip into mixture, filling spoon full. Dip second teaspoon into cold water, then use it to push mixture out of first spoon into simmering fish stock. Cook several at one time but do not crowd. Cook 12 to 15 minutes, turning once. Remove with slotted spoon and put into bowl with cold water to stop cooking. Drain; put in lightly greased casserole or in individual shells or ramekins. Brush tops with melted butter. Heat oysters in their own liquid for several minutes or until edges curl. Drain off liquid and spoon oysters around quenelles.

Sauce Bercy (White Wine Sauce)
5 tablespoons butter
1/4 cup flour
2 cups fish stock from quenelles
1/2 teaspoon salt
1/8 teaspoon white pepper
2 egg yolks
1 shallot
2 tablespoons dry white wine
1 tablespoon fresh lemon juice

Melt 4 tablespoons of the butter in saucepan, add flour, stir and cook 2 minutes. Add fish stock (strain and use stock quenelles were cooked in). Cook on medium heat, stirring constantly, until thick. Add salt and pepper. Beat yolks, add several tablespoons of hot sauce, stir in; then return all to sauce, stirring as you add. Heat thoroughly, do not boil. Put shallot in processor using steel blade. Process until finely chopped. In another saucepan, combine shallot and wine. Cook until all liquid is evaporated; add to sauce with lemon juice and the remaining 1 tablespoon of butter. Makes about 2 cups of sauce.

When ready to serve, spoon sauce over quenelles and oysters in ramekins. Heat in 350° oven 15 to 20 minutes or until thoroughly heated.

Note Recipe will serve 8 as a first course.

QUENELLES DE POISSON II
Fish Dumplings with White Wine Sauce
Serves 6

4 tablespoons butter
1/4 teaspoon salt
1/2 cup water
1/2 cup flour
2 whole eggs
1/2 pound flounder or haddock fillets
3 egg whites
4 cups fish stock (see Basics) or water

In saucepan bring butter, 1/8 teaspoon salt and the water to boil. As soon as butter is melted, remove saucepan from heat, add flour at once and beat vigorously with wooden spoon until thoroughly blended. Return saucepan to heat and continue beating until mixture forms a ball which leaves the sides of pan. Keep heating and beating 2 or 3 minutes longer, thus evaporating excess moisture. Remove from heat, spoon into processor using steel blade. With processor on, add eggs through feed tube, 1 at a time. Spoon paste into bowl, press wax paper or plastic wrap on top to prevent crust from forming. Chill 30 minutes.

Dry fillets on paper towels, cut into 2-inch lengths. Put fish in processor using steel blade. Process until ground. Add chilled choux paste and remaining 1/8 teaspoon salt; mix thoroughly. With processor on add egg whites, one at a time. The pastry must be stiff enough to hold its shape when lifted in a spoon. If paste is too firm add part of an extra egg white. Test consistency by poaching a quenelle. Take a teaspoonful of the mixture, place on lightly floured wax paper and with floured hand roll into a cylinder about 2-1/2 inches long and 1 inch in diameter. Slip quenelle into a saucepan containing 3 to 4 inches of barely simmering fish stock or water. Poach, uncovered, 15 to 20 minutes, always keeping the stock just at simmering point. Cook several at once but do not crowd pan. Remove with a slotted spoon. Plunge in bowl of cold water, then drain on paper towels. Quenelle should be light and hold its shape. Repeat with remaining dumpling mixture.

Sauce Vin Blanc (White Wine Sauce with Cream)
1 carrot
1 6-inch celery stalk
1/2 small onion
4 tablespoons butter
2 tablespoons flour
1 cup fish stock from quenelles
1/2 cup dry white wine
1 bay leaf
Pinch of thyme
1 egg yolk
1/4 cup heavy cream
Salt to taste
White pepper to taste
Few drops fresh lemon juice

Cut carrot and celery into 2-inch lengths; cut onion in half. Put all in processor using steel blade. Process until coarsely chopped. Melt 2 tablespoons of the butter in saucepan, add vegetables and cook on moderate heat 5 to 10 minutes or until tender. Stir in flour and cook for 2 minutes, stirring constantly. Gradually add fish stock (strain and use stock quenelles were cooked in) and wine, still stirring. Bring to simmer; add bay leaf and thyme; simmer 20 to 30 minutes; strain into a clean saucepan. You should have about 1 cup of lightly thickened sauce. Beat egg yolk and cream together; stir in several tablespoons of hot sauce; then return all to saucepan, stirring as you add. Bring back to simmer; simmer 1 minute. Taste for seasoning, adding salt and pepper if needed. Add a few drops of lemon juice. Lastly stir in remaining butter, a tablespoon at a time. Serve immediately. If necessary to keep warm, dot top with butter to prevent film forming and set saucepan in pan of almost simmering water. Makes about 1-1/2 cups of sauce.

When ready to serve, place quenelles in lightly buttered serving dish or individual shells. Spoon sauce over. Heat in 375° oven 20 minutes.

Note Recipe will serve 8 as a first course.

Poultry
Volaille

CRÊPES DE POULARDE
Chicken Crêpes
Serves 6

Sauce Suprême
3 tablespoons butter
3 tablespoons flour
3/4 cup chicken stock, see Basics
3/4 cup half-and-half cream
1/4 teaspoon salt
Dash of black pepper
1/4 cup white vermouth

1/2 medium onion
4 stalks celery
2 tablespoons butter
2-1/2 cups diced cooked chicken
16 Entrée Crêpes, page 28

Melt butter in saucepan. Add flour, stir in and cook 2 minutes. Add stock and cream. Cook on medium heat, stirring constantly until thick. Add salt, pepper and vermouth.

Cut onion in half; cut celery into 2-inch lengths. Put both in processor using steel blade; process until coarsely chopped. Sauté onion and celery in butter about 5 minutes or until tender. Combine onion mixture, chicken and half the Sauce Suprême. Place a big spoonful of filling on lower third of crêpe; roll. Arrange crêpes in lightly buttered baking dish. Pour remaining sauce on top. Bake in 350° oven 20 to 25 minutes.

Variation For curry filling, omit vermouth and add 1 teaspoon curry powder to sauce.

SUPRÊMES DE VOLAILLE À LA MILANAISE
Chicken Breasts with Parmesan Cheese
Serves 4

4 chicken breast halves
Salt to taste
Black pepper to taste
Flour
1 egg
1 tablespoon water
1/2 cup fine white bread crumbs, see Basics
1/2 cup grated Parmesan cheese, see Basics
6 to 8 tablespoons clarified butter, see Basics

Skin and debone the breasts or buy them deboned; season with salt and pepper. Place between two pieces of wax paper; pound with a mallet to flatten. One at a time, roll them in flour and shake off excess. Beat egg with water and combine crumbs and cheese. Dip chicken in egg, then roll in crumbs mixture. Lay on wax paper and place in refrigerator 15 to 20 minutes or several hours. Sauté in clarified butter until brown and springy to the pressure of your finger (about 6 to 8 minutes). Remove to warm platter.

Beurre Noisette (Brown Butter Sauce)
4 parsley sprigs
4 tablespoons clarified butter, see Basics
1 tablespoon fresh lemon juice

Put parsley sprigs in processor using steel blade. Process until parsley is minced. Add butter to skillet where chicken was sautéed. Heat on medium-high heat until light brown. Remove from heat, add parsley and lemon juice; pour over chicken and serve at once.

SUPRÊMES À LA BERNOISE
Chicken Breasts with Cream Sauce
Serves 4

4 chicken breast halves
Salt
Black pepper
Flour
1 egg
1 teaspoon water
3/4 cup fine bread crumbs, see Basics
4 tablespoons clarified butter, see Basics
1/2 clove garlic
1/4 medium onion
1 cup half-and-half cream
3 sprigs parsley
1 bay leaf
1/2 stalk celery
1 teaspoon fresh lemon juice
4 thin slices Swiss cheese, about 3 by 2-1/2 inches

Skin and debone chicken breasts; sprinkle with salt and pepper; coat with flour. Beat egg with water. Dip each breast into egg and then coat with bread crumbs. Place on platter and chill in refrigerator 30 minutes to 1 hour. Melt 3 tablespoons of the clarified butter in heavy skillet and sauté chicken on each side 3 to 4 minutes or until light brown. Put garlic in processor using steel blade; process until fine. Leave garlic in processor; add onion and process until coarsely chopped. Heat remaining tablespoon of butter in heavy saucepan; add onion mixture; sauté 3 to 4 minutes. Add cream, parsley, bay leaf and celery; simmer 10 minutes.

Place chicken breasts in casserole; top each with a slice of Swiss cheese. Strain cream sauce; add lemon juice and add salt to taste. Pour around chicken pieces. Place in 375° oven 12 to 15 minutes or until cheese melts. Serve immediately. Or, dish may be prepared 2 or 3 hours in advance. Prepare, cover with plastic wrap or aluminum foil. Uncover to heat.

SUPRÊMES AUX CHAMPIGNONS
Chicken Breasts with Mushroom Sauce
Serves 4

4 chicken breast halves
Salt
Black pepper
Flour
2 shallots
1/4 pound mushrooms
5 tablespoons clarified butter, see Basics
2 teaspoons flour
3 tablespoons white wine
1/2 cup chicken stock, see Basics

Skin and debone chicken breasts or buy them already deboned. Put meat between wax paper and pound with mallet to flatten. Cut each piece in half lengthwise. Trim off raggy edges. Season with salt and pepper; coat with flour. Place on plate, cover with plastic wrap and refrigerate until firm.

Make sauce while chicken chills. Put shallots in processor using steel blade. Process until fine; remove to bowl. Using slicing disc in processor, put mushrooms through feed tube, placing them on their sides. Process till sliced. Melt 2 tablespoons clarified butter in saucepan; add the shallots and cook on low heat 3 to 4 minutes. Add mushrooms, stir and cook 2 minutes. Add flour and stir in. Add wine and chicken stock. Cook several minutes. Add salt to taste.

Melt remaining butter in heavy skillet. Add chicken fillets and sauté until brown; turn and brown second side. Total cooking time should be about 5 minutes. Remove to dinner plates and spoon sauce over each serving.

Note Chicken fillets may be prepared 2 or 3 hours in advance. Put in ramekins, add mushroom sauce, then cover until ready to heat. Uncover and heat in 350° oven 15 minutes. If made earlier, refrigerate until ready to heat and increase time in oven to 25 minutes.

POULET SAUTÉ NORMANDE
Chicken with Cream
Serves 4 to 5

2-1/2 pounds fryer chicken pieces
3 tablespoons clarified butter, see Basics
2 shallots
1/4 cup cognac
Salt to taste
White pepper to taste
3/4 cup chicken stock, see Basics
Bouquet garni, below
1 tablespoon beurre manié, see Basics
2 to 3 tablespoons heavy cream

Skin chicken, dry thoroughly and brown in butter over medium heat. Put shallots in processor using steel blade. Process until finely chopped. Add shallots to chicken and sauté a few minutes longer. Add cognac, then flame. (Stand back from skillet when you flame cognac.) Let flame burn out. Season with salt and pepper. Add stock and bouquet garni. Cover and simmer 20 minutes. Remove chicken from pan and keep warm. Strain sauce; return to pan; add beurre manié and cream. Stir constantly and continue heating 2 to 3 minutes or until thickened. Adjust seasoning if necessary and spoon sauce over chicken.

Bouquet garni Tie in cheesecloth 1/2 stalk celery, 2 sprigs parsley, 1 bay leaf, 1/4 teaspoon thyme and 2 peppercorns.

COQ AU VIN
Chicken Cooked in Wine
Serves 4 to 6

This dish is almost better if cooked one day, refrigerated and reheated the next day.

1 broiler chicken, 2-1/2 to 3 pounds, quartered, or
    3 pounds fryer pieces
1/4 pound sliced bacon
2 tablespoons butter
2 shallots
1 clove garlic
1 cup chicken stock, see Basics
2 cups burgundy wine
Bouquet garni, below
1/2 teaspoon salt
1/8 teaspoon black pepper
8 to 10 small white onions, peeled
1/2 pound small mushrooms
2 tablespoons beurre manié, see Basics

A broiler will serve 4 people. Three pounds of meaty chicken parts (breasts, thighs and legs) will serve 6. If desired bone chicken parts. Dice bacon and fry on medium heat to render fat. Remove bacon bits, add butter. Dry chicken with paper towel, add to hot fat and brown lightly on all sides. Put shallots and garlic in processor using steel blade and process until minced; add to skillet with chicken. Add bacon, stock, wine, bouquet garni, salt, pepper and onions. Cover and simmer 45 minutes or until chicken is tender. Add mushrooms after 30 minutes.

To serve remove chicken, onions and mushrooms to hot platter with a slotted spoon. Remove and discard bouquet garni. Thicken liquid by stirring in beurre manié and simmering for a few minutes. Spoon some sauce over chicken. Serve remaining sauce in bowl.

Bouquet garni Tie in cheesecloth 1/2 stalk celery, 2 sprigs parsley, 1 bay leaf, 1 sprig thyme or 1/4 teaspoon dry thyme leaves, and 1 leek or 1 green onion (trim leek or onion leaving about 1/2 inch of green top).

POULARDE FARCI AU FOIE
Chicken Stuffed with Livers
Serves 6

A roasting hen stuffed with sautéed chicken livers and served with a peppery sauce. It's best to make the sauce the day before since it does require time to brown, simmer and strain the vegetables.

1 pound chicken livers
6 tablespoons butter
1/2 teaspoon sweet basil
1/4 cup cognac
Salt to taste
Black pepper to taste
1 whole roasting chicken, 5 to 7 pounds
24 white boiling onions, peeled
16 to 18 cherry tomatoes

Remove any fat from livers; sauté in 4 tablespoons of the butter 5 minutes; sprinkle sweet basil over all. Pour on cognac, heat and then flame. Remove from heat, season with salt and pepper. Sprinkle cavity of hen with salt and pepper, fill with livers. Tie legs together and fold wings back. Melt remaining 2 tablespoons butter, brush chicken thoroughly. Roast in 425° oven 40 minutes; reduce temperature to 350° and cook 40 minutes longer. Brush several times with melted butter. If legs or wings become too brown, cover that area with aluminum foil. To test for doneness, press thigh of chicken, protecting finger with paper towel. Meat should give under the pressure.

Thirty minutes before serving, cook onions in salted water for 5 minutes; drain, rinse and sauté in butter 15 to 20 minutes or until tender. Add unpeeled tomatoes to onions in skillet; sauté 5 to 6 minutes. Put hen on platter. Arrange onions and tomatoes around hen. Serve Sauce Diable separately.

Sauce Diable (Peppery Brown Sauce)
Sauce Demi-Glace, page 127
2 shallots
2 tablespoons butter
1/2 cup white wine
2 tablespoons vinegar
Black pepper
Cayenne pepper

Make Demi-Glace Sauce. Put shallots in processor using steel blade; process until chopped. Put shallots and butter in saucepan, cook 2 minutes without browning. Add wine and vinegar, boil rapidly until reduced to 3 or 4 tablespoons. Add to sauce; season with peppers until spicy. Serve hot. Makes 1-1/2 to 2 cups of sauce.

POULARDE RÔTI
Roast Chicken
Serves 4

This poulard rôti is stuffed with boiled eggs and served with a sauce suprême. The eggs are partially cooked, peeled and rolled in chopped parsley. The sauce is made with chicken stock and enriched with crème fraîche.

1 whole roasting chicken, 4 to 5 pounds
Salt
Black pepper
8 sprigs parsley
6 small eggs
3 tablespoons melted butter
3 thin slices salt pork

Remove giblets from body of chicken and set aside (see note below). Rinse chicken with cold water; drain and pat dry with paper towels. Sprinkle body cavity with salt and pepper. Place parsley in processor using steel blade. Process until fine, remove to flat dish. Place eggs in saucepan. Add cold water to cover by 1 inch. Bring to boil; reduce heat and simmer 5 minutes. Drain off hot water; cover with cold water to stop cooking. Peel eggs and roll in chopped parsley; stuff into cavity. Truss chicken with needle and thread or use skewers to close body cavity; tie legs together with string. Brush with melted butter; cover white meat with strips of salt pork. Place chicken on broiler rack slightly tilted to one side. Pour about 1-1/2 cups water into broiling pan. Bake in 425° oven for 40 minutes; remove pork slices and reduce heat to 325°. Bake 20 minutes longer or until done. To test for doneness, push thickest part of thigh with finger (protect finger with paper towel). Meat should give to your pressure. Turn chicken about every 20 minutes and brush with additional butter. Let chicken rest 15 minutes before carving. Serve with Sauce Suprême.

Sauce Suprême
4 tablespoons butter
1/4 cup flour
2 cups chicken stock, see Basics
Salt to taste
1/4 cup crème fraîche, see Basics
1 tablespoon fresh lemon juice

Melt butter in saucepan; stir in flour. Cook and stir for a few minutes; add stock; continue cooking and stirring until thickened; add salt, crème fraîche and lemon juice. Makes about 2 cups of sauce.

Note The chicken gizzard and liver may be cooked and added to sauce. Put in saucepan and cover with water. Add 1/2 teaspoon salt, 1/2 onion and 2 sprigs parsley; simmer about 25 minutes. Chop and add to Sauce Suprême.

POULARDE SAINTE HÉLÈNE
Chicken with Veal Dumplings
Serves 6

Veal quenelles or dumplings accompany this braised chicken. It's much easier and quicker to make the paste and grind the veal for the quenelles using the processor.

1 whole roasting chicken, 3 to 4 pounds
2 tablespoons oil
4 tablespoons flour
1/4 cup cognac
3 onions, quartered
2 cloves garlic, halved
2 cups red wine
1 cup chicken stock, see Basics
1/8 teaspoon thyme
Bouquet garni, below
1-1/2 teaspoons salt
Black pepper to taste
1/2 pound mushrooms
2 cups water
1 tablespoon butter
2 tablespoons red wine
2 sprigs parsley

Remove any fat from chicken; rinse with water, drain well and pat dry. Heat oil in large saucepan and brown whole chicken. Sprinkle flour over all, then pour cognac on fowl and set aflame. Let flame burn out. Add onions, garlic, the 2 cups wine, stock, thyme, bouquet garni, 1 teaspoon of salt and the pepper. Bring to boil, reduce heat to simmer and cook 50 to 60 minutes or until done. Liquid will not completely cover fowl, so turn from side to side as it cooks. Test for doneness by piercing thigh with fork; if juices run clear, chicken is done. Remove bouquet garni at the end of cooking period.

While chicken is cooking, prepare quenelles as directed in following recipe. Then wash mushrooms and cut off stems even with the cap. Combine mushrooms, water, butter and remaining 1/2 teaspoon salt in saucepan. Simmer 2 minutes and remove from heat.

Put chicken on warm serving platter; strain cooking liquid and skim off fat. Drain mushrooms, put in medium-size skillet. Add quenelles; sprinkle the 2 tablespoons red wine over all. Add 1 cup of the strained sauce and heat. Pour mushroom-quenelle sauce around chicken. Put parsley in processor using steel blade; process until chopped. Sprinkle parsley over chicken and serve remaining sauce on the side.

Quenelles de Veau (Veal Dumplings)
4 tablespoons butter
1/2 cup water
1/4 teaspoon salt
1/2 cup flour
2 eggs
1/2 pound lean veal
1/2 teaspoon salt
Dash of white pepper
2 egg whites
1 to 4 tablespoons chilled heavy cream
3 cups chicken stock (see Basics) or water
Additional salt to taste

In saucepan bring butter, water and 1/4 teaspoon salt to boil. As soon as butter melts, remove saucepan from heat, add flour at once and beat vigorously with wooden spoon until thoroughly blended. Return saucepan to heat and continue beating until mixture forms a ball which leaves the sides of pan. Remove from heat; put in processor using steel blade. With processor on, add eggs 1 at a time. When paste is thoroughly blended, spoon into bowl. Press wax paper or plastic wrap on top of paste and refrigerate. Chill thoroughly (about 1 hour).

Cube veal, put in processor using steel blade. Process until veal is ground. Add chilled paste to veal and process until thoroughly blended. Continue mixing and gradually add 1/2 teaspoon salt, the pepper and egg whites. Then add cream 1 table-spoon at a time. Try to beat in as much cream as possible but still retain enough body so that the paste can be shaped and poached without disintegrating.

In heavy 2- or 3-quart saucepan heat chicken stock or water to simmer. Add salt to taste. Form quenelles by taking a spoonful of the paste and rolling with the palm of one hand on a lightly floured board to make cylindrical shapes about 2 inches long and 1 inch in diameter. Slip into the broth. Let quenelles poach uncovered 12 to 15 minutes. They will swell almost double and roll over easily. Remove with slotted spoon and drain on paper towels.

Bouquet garni Tie string around 3 sprigs parsley, 1 bay leaf and 1 sprig thyme. Or substitute 1/8 teaspoon dry thyme and tie with parsley and bay leaf in cheesecloth.

CANARD À L'ORANGE
Duck with Orange Sauce
Serves 3

Duck with Orange Sauce takes some effort, but it's worth it. The sauce takes time to prepare, so plan ahead and have sauce prepared to its final stage. Serve wild rice or a combination of wild and brown rice with the duck.

1 duck, 4 to 5 pounds
Salt
Black pepper
2 tablespoons honey
2 tablespoons water

Remove giblets from duck; then remove wishbone. To remove wishbone, put duck on its back. Pull neck skin back over the breast meat. Using a sharp knife, reach into the neck cavity and cut through meat around wishbone. With your fingers, pull the wishbone from the meat, break it off and discard. Stand duck on its legs in sink and scald with boiling water. (Hot water swells the skin and opens the pores so that fat drains out during cooking.) Sprinkle well with salt and pepper; place on rack of roasting pan. Cook in 425° oven 50 minutes; reduce heat to 325° and cook 25 minutes longer. Combine honey and water; brush duck generously last 10 minutes of cooking time. Let rest 10 minutes; then carve (directions follow).

Sauce Bigarade (Orange Sauce)
2 tablespoons sugar
2 tablespoons vinegar
Sauce Demi-Glace, page 127
2 oranges
1 lemon
2 tablespoons fresh orange juice
1 teaspoon fresh lemon juice
2 tablespoons cognac
1 tablespoon Madeira

While duck is cooking prepare Sauce Bigarade. Combine sugar and vinegar; boil until vinegar evaporates and sugar turns light brown. Add Sauce Demi-Glace. Remove zest from 1 orange and the lemon, cut into julienne strips. Put in a separate saucepan, cover with water and bring to boil (blanching removes bitterness); drain. Peel oranges with knife, cutting deep enough to remove all the white membrane; separate into sections. Combine orange sections with one quarter of Sauce Demi-Glace and simmer 5 to 10 minutes. Add orange and lemon zest and juices to remaining sauce; heat thoroughly. Add cognac and Madeira.

To Carve Duck

Cut completely around the body of the duck at the top of legs and wings. Carefully remove breast meat. Remove legs at the body. Separate thighs from legs. Cut off wings. Place breast fillets on cutting board. Slice thinly and put back in place. Arrange thighs, legs and wings where they belong on the carcass. Press meat to carcass with hands.

Place duck on ovenproof platter and heat in very hot oven to rewarm. Lift some of the shredded zest from sauce and strew over carved duck. Arrange glazed orange sections on or around duck. Serve sauce separately.

Meat
Viande

BOEUF BOURGUIGNON
Beef Stew in Red Wine
Serves 6

3 pounds boneless chuck
3 tablespoons bacon drippings or oil
1/2 clove garlic
1 shallot
1 medium onion
1 bay leaf
Pinch of thyme
3 sprigs parsley
1-1/2 cups red wine
1/2 cup beef stock, see Basics
1/8 pound salt pork (2 slices)
1 tablespoon tomato sauce
2 tablespoons beurre manié, see Basics

Cut meat into 1-1/2- to 2-inch cubes, removing any excess fat. Heat bacon drippings in skillet; add meat and brown on all sides, stirring frequently. Put garlic and shallot in processor using steel blade. Process until minced, add to beef. Slice onion in processor using slicing disc; add to meat along with remaining ingredients except beurre manié. Bring to a boil, cover and reduce heat. Barely simmer 1-1/2 to 2 hours or until meat is fork tender. Remove bay leaf and parsley. Add beurre manié, stir and simmer a few minutes longer or until slightly thickened. Serve with boiled potatoes, rice or noodles.

ESCOFFIER DE BOEUF
Roast Beef in Wine
Serves 6 to 8

1 rump roast of beef, 3 to 5 pounds
3 cups red wine
1 clove garlic
2 onions
2 carrots
2 stalks celery
3 tablespoons butter
1/2 teaspoon salt
Black pepper to taste
Dash of nutmeg
2 tablespoons beurre manié, see Basics

Put roast in a deep bowl; add wine and marinate 5 hours or overnight. If wine does not cover roast, turn several times during marinating process. Put garlic in processor using steel blade; process until very fine. Cut onions into fourths, cut carrots and celery into 2-inch lengths; put all into processor with garlic. Process until coarsely chopped. Melt butter in heavy casserole, add vegetables and brown lightly. Add salt, pepper and nutmeg. Add roast and wine, cover and cook in 350° oven 2 to 3 hours or until tender. Remove roast, strain broth and return to casserole; thicken with beurre manié. Slice roast and serve sauce in separate bowl.

BOEUF À LA MODE
Beef Braised in Red Wine
Serves 10 to 14

A great meat to serve family or friends, this roast is tender, well-flavored and has an excellent sauce. It could be completely prepared a day in advance, refrigerated and then well heated before serving.

1 rump roast of beef, 5 to 6 pounds
3 tablespoons bacon drippings or oil
4 ounces bacon
1 cracked veal knuckle
1 split pig's foot
1 medium onion
3 carrots
2 stalks celery
2 cloves garlic, halved
1 tablespoon thyme
2 bay leaves
3 sprigs parsley
2 whole cloves
2 teaspoons salt
4 peppercorns
2-1/2 cups red wine
2-1/2 cups beef stock, see Basics
2 tablespoons cornstarch
3 tablespoons water
Additional parsley

Wipe roast dry with paper towels. Heat drippings or oil in large casserole, add roast and brown on all sides. Dice bacon, put in separate saucepan, cover with water. Simmer 10 minutes, drain; add to roast. Add knuckle and pig's foot. Slice onion, carrots and celery in processor using slicing disc. Add to roast. Add remaining ingredients except cornstarch and water. Bring to simmer on top of range. Cover tightly and set in 325° oven 3 to 4 hours, or until tender when pierced with sharp-pronged fork. Turn meat several times during cooking period.

Remove meat, strain braising liquid, skim off fat, return to casserole. Boil rapidly to reduce liquid to approximately 3-1/2 cups. Taste for salt. Combine cornstarch and water, stir in. Return meat to casserole, heat 5 to 10 minutes, barely simmering. Remove meat, slice and arrange on platter. Garnish with parsley. Spoon small amount of sauce over meat. Serve remaining sauce in bowl.

Note Beef may be marinated 6 to 24 hours if desired. Place in glass or porcelain bowl and add ingredients, starting with onion and continuing through red wine. Cover and place in refrigerator. Turn meat several times. Before browning, drain and dry well on paper towels. Continue as directed in recipe.

BOEUF MODE EN GELÉE
Braised Beef in Aspic
Serves 10 to 14

This elegant dish requires two days of preparation and can be completely finished the day before you plan to serve it. Serve this roast with its glistening aspic at your next buffet dinner.

Boeuf à la Mode, preceding
1 10-1/2-ounce can beef consommé
1 package unflavored gelatin
Salt
Black pepper
1/4 cup port or brandy, optional
6 to 8 boiling onions, peeled and cooked
Watercress or parsley

Prepare beef according to Boeuf à la Mode recipe up to the point of adding cornstarch and water. Add enough water to consommé to make 1-1/2 cups, add gelatin and let stand until gelatin softens. Pour gelatin into braising liquid and heat until gelatin dissolves. Taste and add salt and pepper if needed. Add port or brandy, cool. Select a mold large enough to hold meat and onions. Slice beef into serving pieces and arrange in mold with onions. Half fill mold with gelée. Place in refrigerator until set.

Do not return remaining gelée to refrigerator. When ready to coat remaining meat, pour small amount (about 1/2 cup) of gelée in metal measuring cup, set in ice water and stir constantly until gelée gets very syrupy. Spoon slowly over meat. Chill until ready to serve. Set mold in hot water for a few moments, unmold in hand and quickly place right side up on serving platter.

Meanwhile chill remaining gelée in a flat pan and chop into 1/8-inch cubes, spoon around roast. Garnish with watercress or parsley.

ESTOUFFADE DE BOEUF À LA PROVENÇALE

Casserole of Beef with Wine and Olives

Serves 6 to 8

Marinade
1 carrot
1 onion
3 to 4 stalks celery
1/2 cup olive oil or other oil
1/2 cup white wine
1/4 cup wine vinegar
5 sprigs parsley
2 cloves garlic
Pinch of thyme
1 bay leaf
6 peppercorns
1/2 teaspoon salt

3 pounds lean beef (bottom round, rump or chuck)
3 tablespoons bacon drippings
1/8 pound salt pork
4 carrots
3 cloves garlic
3/4 cup pitted green olives
2 tablespoons beurre manié, see Basics
10 ounces thin noodles
3 tablespoons butter

To make marinade, cut carrot into 2-inch lengths, cut onion into quarters. Put both in processor using steel blade. Process until coarsely chopped. Remove to bowl. Cut celery into 2-inch lengths, add to processor using steel blade; process until coarsely chopped. Heat oil in saucepan, add carrot, onion and celery; cook stirring constantly until light brown. Add remaining marinade ingredients and simmer for a few minutes. Cool.

Cut meat across the grain into 1/4- to 1/2-inch-thick slices. Place in bowl, cover with cooled marinade, refrigerate for 24 hours. Remove meat from marinade, drain and dry on paper towels. Heat bacon drippings in heavy skillet and brown meat on both sides. Strain marinade and add to skillet, adding water and wine if necessary to cover meat completely. Slice salt pork and add. Cut carrots in half crosswise and add. Put garlic in processor using steel blade. Process until very fine. Leave garlic in processor, add olives and process until coarsely chopped. Add to skillet. Bring mixture to boil; cover with tight-fitting lid and cook in 275° oven 1 hour or until meat is tender. Liquid should be barely boiling. Remove salt pork and discard. Skim fat from surface. (If necessary, pour all liquid into a deep narrow bowl. Fat can be spooned from top more easily.) When ready to serve add beurre manié to meat and broth. Stir and heat until meat is hot and liquid is thickened. Cook noodles al dente; toss with butter.

To serve put meat slices in center of platter and noodles at each end. Spoon small amount of sauce over meat. Serve remaining sauce in bowl.

RÔTI DE BOEUF NIVERNAISE
Eye of Round Roast with Vegetables
Serves 8

An eye of round roast is solid lean meat. It requires several hours of cooking, holds its shape well and produces firm slices.

1 eye of round roast, 3 to 4 pounds
4 tablespoons butter
3 tablespoons oil
2 carrots
2 onions
1-1/2 cups chicken stock, see Basics
1 bay leaf
3 sprigs parsley
5 peppercorns
2 thick slices bacon or salt pork
1 teaspoon salt
1 tablespoon tomato paste
4 to 6 tablespoons beurre manié, see Basics
16 small whole cooked new potatoes
16 small whole cooked onions
Oil or a mixture of equal parts of oil and butter
4 tomatoes
Additional salt

Sauté roast briskly in 2 tablespoons each of the butter and oil. Slice carrots and onions in processor using slicing disc. In another saucepan, lightly brown carrots and onions in remaining butter and oil. Add roast with stock, bay leaf, parsley and peppercorns. Place bacon in saucepan, cover with water, simmer 10 minutes, drain. (This removes smoked flavor.) If salt pork is used, there is no need to simmer. Add bacon or salt pork, the 1 teaspoon salt and tomato paste to roast. Bring to boil, cover and place in 300° oven 2 hours or until tender. Liquid should barely boil while in oven. Remove roast to platter, lightly cover with foil and put in warm oven to keep hot. Strain cooking liquid and skim off fat. Return liquid to saucepan. Thicken with beurre manié using 2 tablespoons per cup of sauce. If a thicker sauce is desired, add more. Heat and stir (with a wire whisk if possible) until smooth and slightly thickened.

Just before serving prepare vegetables. Brown potatoes and onions in separate skillets in hot oil or a combination of oil and butter, using enough oil to cover bottoms of skillets. Cut tomatoes in half crosswise, remove seeds, sprinkle with salt and sauté in hot oil until tender. Surround roast with vegetables. Serve sauce on the side.

PAUPIETTES DE BOEUF
Pork-Stuffed Beef Rolls
Serves 4 to 5

2 pounds round steak (1/2 inch thick)
Salt
Black pepper
1/2 clove garlic
1/2 medium onion
1 tablespoon butter
9 sprigs parsley

1 pork chop
1/2 slice bread
1 egg
1/8 teaspoon thyme
Dash of allspice
1/4 teaspoon salt
2 or 3 tablespoons cooking oil
1-1/2 cups beef stock, see Basics
1 cup dry white wine
1 bay leaf
1 tablespoon Dijon mustard
2 tablespoons beurre manié, see Basics

Debone steak; cut into six equal rectangles. If time permits chill in freezer until firm before proceeding. Cut each rectangle crosswise, making two rectangles 1/4 inch thick. You will have 12 slices in all. Salt and pepper each slice. Put garlic in processor using steel blade. Process until very fine. Cut onion in half, put in processor with garlic; process until coarsely chopped. Melt butter in saucepan; add onion mixture and sauté 5 to 7 minutes or until tender. Remove to bowl. Put 6 sprigs of the parsley in processor. Process till finely chopped; add to onion mixture. Trim pork from bone. Put lean pork, 2 tablespoons pork fat, lean trimming from steak, and bread in processor with garlic using steel blade. Process until mixture is smooth. Add egg, thyme, allspice, 1/4 teaspoon salt and a dash of pepper. Again process until blended. Add to onion mixture in bowl; mix. On each slice of meat, spoon 1 tablespoon filling on lower third of slice. Roll the meat around the stuffing; tie both ends with string. Heat oil in heavy casserole; brown rolls lightly on all sides. Combine stock and wine, pour over rolls. Add remaining parsley and bay leaf; cover and bring to boil. Put in 325° oven and cook for 1 to 1-1/2 hours or until tender. Remove rolls from sauce, cut and remove string. (Sauce may be strained if desired.) Add mustard and beurre manié to sauce, stir and bring to boil. Arrange rolls on serving dish; spoon some sauce over rolls. Serve remaining sauce in bowl.

Roulades de Boeuf (Bread-Stuffed Beef Rolls) Substitute the following for the pork filling.

1 medium onion
8 sprigs parsley
1 cup bread stuffing mix, or your favorite bread
    stuffing
4 tablespoons melted butter

Cut onion into quarters. Put in processor using steel blade. Process until coarsely chopped, remove to bowl. Put parsley in processor; finely chop. Add parsley to onion. Combine stuffing mix and butter. On each meat rectangle spread a layer of onion-parsley mixture then a layer of bread stuffing. Roll up, tie and proceed as in above recipe.

CARBONNADE
Braised Beef in Beer
Serves 6 to 8

Beef braised in onions and beer sounds like a strong-flavored, hearty dish. Not so; it is a delicate-flavored stew. The long, slow cooking removes the strong onion flavor and the beer helps to tenderize the meat.

3 pounds boneless pot roast
2 tablespoons butter
3 medium onions
2 teaspoons flour
1 teaspoon sugar
1 12-ounce can light beer
1/2 cup beef stock, see Basics
Bouquet garni, below
2 tablespoons beurre manié, see Basics

Slice meat into 1/2-inch-thick slices. Heat butter in heavy saucepan, add sliced meat and brown on both sides; remove when brown. Cut onions in half and slice in processor using slicing disc. Add onions to pan and cook, stirring frequently, until slightly browned. Add flour and sugar; stir constantly until well browned. Add beer, beef stock and bouquet garni. Return meat to pan. Bring to boil, cover and simmer 1 to 1-1/2 hours or until meat is tender. Or cook in 300° oven for same period. Remove meat and keep hot. Remove and discard bouquet garni. Add beurre manié to liquid in pan, stir with whisk and cook until slightly thickened. Spoon a little sauce over meat, serve remaining sauce in bowl.

Bouquet garni Tie in cheesecloth 1/2 stalk celery, 2 sprigs parsley, 1 bay leaf and 1 sprig thyme or 1/4 teaspoon dry thyme.

BOEUF À LA NORMANDE
Beef with Oysters and Mushrooms
Serves 4

2 pounds round steak, 1/2 inch thick
Salt
Black pepper
4 tablespoons clarified butter, see Basics
1 medium onion
1 large carrot
1 clove garlic
1 bay leaf
2 sprigs parsley
1/4 teaspoon thyme
2-1/2 cups chicken stock or beef stock, see Basics
1/2 pound small mushrooms
2 tablespoons beurre manié, see Basics
1 dozen oysters

Cut steak into serving portions and trim excess fat. Season with salt and pepper, brown on both sides in hot butter; remove from skillet. Quarter onion; cut carrot into 2-inch lengths; put in processor with garlic using steel blade. Process until coarsely chopped. Add vegetables to skillet, brown lightly. Return steak to skillet. Add bay leaf, parsley, thyme and chicken or beef stock. Cover and cook at a low boil 1 to 1-1/2 hours or until meat is tender. Remove meat from skillet; strain sauce and spoon off surface fat. Return sauce to skillet, add mushrooms and cook 5 minutes. Add beurre manié, stir until dissolved. Add oysters; immediately add meat. Bring to boil; boil 3 to 4 minutes or until oysters are curled around the edges. Place meat on platter, spoon mushrooms and oysters on each serving. Serve remaining sauce in bowl.

BOEUF WELLINGTON
Beef Tenderloin in Pastry
Serves 6

One of the most elegant meat dishes you can serve. Develop your own expertise at making this pastry-covered beef tenderloin.

Pastry
3 cups flour
1/2 teaspoon salt
14 tablespoons butter, frozen
1/4 cup shortening, frozen
7 tablespoons ice water

1 tenderloin of beef, 2-1/2 to 3 pounds
Salt
Black pepper
1 tablespoon cognac
2 to 3 slices bacon
3 to 6 ounces pâté de foie gras or liver pâté
3 to 4 truffles, optional
1 egg
1 teaspoon milk

In processor using steel blade put flour, salt, butter and shortening. Process until mixture has consistency of coarse cornmeal. While machine is running, add water slowly through feed tube until mixture forms a ball. If mixture is not moist enough, add more ice water, 1/2 teaspoon at a time, until ball forms. Wrap in wax paper; chill.

Rub beef with salt and pepper; sprinkle cognac over all. Lay bacon on top and tie with string to secure. Place meat on rack in roasting pan. Roast in 450° oven, allowing 10 to 15 minutes per pound for rare and 20 to 25 minutes per pound for medium. Remove bacon; let beef cool completely. Spread the pâté over sides and top of meat. Cut truffles and press into pâté along top. Roll pastry into rectangle large enough to wrap tenderloin. Wrap meat, trim edges. Moisten edges to make a good seal. Roll out pastry trimmings and cut into narrow strips. Lay strips across dough-wrapped beef in lattice pattern. Make three vents in top. Combine egg and milk; brush this mixture over all. Bake in 425° oven 20 minutes or until pastry is golden brown.

Note Beef may be prepared in advance and refrigerated in its pastry. Let stand at room temperature 20 to 30 minutes before baking.

NAVARIN PRINTANIER
Ragout of Lamb
Serves 6 to 8

Navarin Printanier is a well-flavored lamb stew containing fresh vegetables. The processor does the chopping and the vegetables can be varied according to what is available at the market.

1 shoulder of lamb, 3 to 4 pounds
3 tablespoons bacon drippings or oil
1 clove garlic
2 medium onions
2 tablespoons flour
2 cups beef stock, see Basics
1 teaspoon salt
Black pepper to taste
1 sprig rosemary or 1/4 teaspoon dry rosemary
1 bay leaf
1 pound new potatoes
6 to 8 small carrots
Few baby turnips
1 pound fresh green peas

Cut lamb into squares. Heat drippings in heavy saucepan, add lamb and cook until lightly brown; remove from pan. Put garlic in processor using steel blade. Process until minced. Cut onions into quarters; put in processor with garlic. Process until onion is coarsely chopped. Add onion and garlic to pan in which lamb was browned, cook for a few minutes. Add flour, stir and heat until you have a light brown roux. Gradually add stock while stirring. Return meat to saucepan. Add salt, pepper, rosemary and bay leaf. Cover and simmer 1 hour or until meat is almost tender. Wash potatoes, scrape carrots, peel turnips. Add to lamb, cook 30 minutes longer. Shell peas and add. Continue cooking until peas are barely tender (10 to 15 minutes for very young peas). If sauce is too thick, add more stock or water.

GIGOT DE PRÉ-SALÉ RÔTI AU SOUBISE
Roast Leg of Lamb with Onion Sauce
Serves 8 to 10

1 leg of lamb, 6 to 7 pounds, boned
2 cloves garlic
Salt
Black pepper

Ask butcher to bone leg of lamb. Trim away any excess fat. Cut garlic into slivers. Make little slits all over the meat using a small sharp knife. Push the garlic slivers into the meat. Tie the leg at intervals with twine. Rub well with salt and pepper. Set on rack in roasting pan. If a meat thermometer is used, it should be inserted about halfway into the thickest part of the meat. Do not let thermometer touch fat. Roast in 350° oven 12 to 15 minutes per pound for pink lamb; 15 to 20 minutes for well done. The thermometer should read 145° to 150° for medium rare and 160° to 165° for well done.

Sauce Soubise (Onion Sauce)
1 medium baking potato
3 medium onions
1/4 pound butter
1 teaspoon salt
Dash of black pepper
2 tablespoons flour
1/2 cup half-and-half cream
2 egg yolks
8 sprigs parsley

While lamb roasts, make sauce. Peel potato; slice potato and onions in processor using slicing disc. Melt 6 tablespoons of the butter in saucepan; add potato, onion, salt and pepper. Cover and cook on medium heat 15 to 20 minutes or until vegetables are tender. Stir occasionally during cooking. Cool 10 to 15 minutes, return to processor using steel blade, and process until smooth. In another saucepan, melt remaining 2 tablespoons butter, stir in flour and cook, stirring constantly, for 2 minutes. Remove from heat; add cream and blend in with whisk. Return to heat, stirring constantly and cooking until mixture is very thick. Beat egg yolks slightly, add a little of the sauce to yolks to warm them, then stir all into sauce. Chop parsley in processor using steel blade; add to sauce along with vegetable purée. Taste for seasoning. Makes about 1-1/2 cups of sauce.

When lamb is done put on carving board, let rest 5 to 10 minutes, carve into 1/4-inch slices. Keep slices in order and arrange on ovenproof serving tray, spreading each slice with Sauce Soubise. Place in 375° oven 10 minutes to reheat.

Note Lamb with sauce may be finished, cooled, covered with plastic wrap and refrigerated until ready to serve. To serve, bring to room temperature, then heat in 400° oven 10 to 15 minutes.

SELLE D'AGNEAU
Roast Saddle of Lamb
Serves 8

1 saddle of lamb, 4 to 6 pounds
Salt
Black pepper
1 clove garlic
3 sprigs parsley
2 shallots or white part of 2 green onions
4 tablespoons butter
1/4 cup soft fresh bread crumbs, see Basics

Rub lamb well with salt and pepper. Insert meat thermometer at least 2 inches into thickest part of meat. (Do not let thermometer touch any fat or bone.) Put lamb, fat side up, in open roasting pan. Roast uncovered and undisturbed in 425° oven for 30 to 45 minutes or until thermometer registers 130°. While lamb is cooking, put garlic in processor using steel blade and process until minced. Add parsley to garlic and process until parsley is chopped; remove to a bowl. Put shallots in processor, still using steel blade, and process till finely chopped. Melt butter; add garlic, parsley, shallots and crumbs. Remove lamb from oven, spread crumb mixture evenly over top; pat down with back of spoon. Roast lamb another 10 minutes or until thermometer registers 140°. Let rest 10 minutes before serving.

JAMBON FARCI ET BRAISÉ
Ham Stuffed with Mushrooms
Serves 8

1 half of ham, 4 to 5 pounds
1/2 medium onion or 4 shallots
1 pound mushrooms
2 tablespoons butter
2 tablespoons Madeira or port
1/2 teaspoon thyme
Pinch of allspice
1 truffle, optional

Sauce au Madère (Madeira Sauce)
1/2 medium onion
1 carrot
2 tablespoons butter or oil
1 cup Madeira
1-1/2 cups beef stock, see Basics
2 sprigs parsley
1 bay leaf
1/4 teaspoon thyme
1 tablespoon arrowroot or cornstarch
2 tablespoons water

Select a semiboneless, partially cooked half of ham. Remove wrapping, place in pan and loosely cover with brown paper sack. Place in 300° oven 30 to 40 minutes or until thoroughly warm. Remove from oven and while still warm remove remaining bone using a thin boning knife.

Cut onion in half, put in processor using steel blade. Process until finely chopped, remove to bowl. Put mushrooms, stems attached, in processor using steel blade. Process until coarsely chopped. Remove juice from mushrooms by putting 1/2 cup chopped mushrooms in corner of clean dishtowel and twisting. Reserve juice. Repeat until moisture has been removed from mushrooms. Cook onion and mushrooms in butter on medium heat 8 to 10 minutes. Add Madeira and boil rapidly until liquid has evaporated. Add thyme and allspice. Chop truffle in processor using steel blade; add. Stand ham on its side on chopping block. Using a very sharp knife, slice into serving slices, leaving the last slice about 1 to 1-1/2 inches thick. Keep slices in order. Spread out cheesecloth and in center begin to reconstruct ham, spreading about 1 tablespoon of stuffing on each slice. Gather cheesecloth firmly around ham and tie with string.

Prepare sauce by cutting onion in half and carrot into 2-inch lengths. Put in processor using steel blade; process until coarsely chopped. In large casserole melt butter, add onion and carrot and cook, stirring frequently, until slightly brown. Add prepared ham, Madeira, stock, parsley, bay leaf and thyme. Bring to simmer, cover and cook in 225° oven about 2 hours. Baste about every 20 minutes. Remove ham and leave in cheesecloth while it cools. Strain liquid, return to saucepan. If necessary, boil rapidly to reduce to about 2 cups. Combine arrowroot with water. Mix thoroughly and add to hot liquid. Let boil for a few minutes. One or 2 tablespoons butter can be added to sauce at last minute if desired. Remove ham from cheesecloth and put on platter. Spoon some sauce over ham. Serve remaining sauce in bowl.

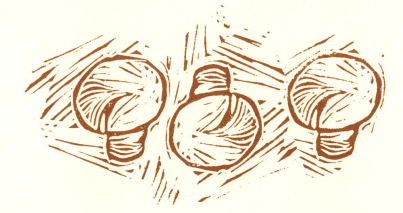

CÔTES DE PORC AU CHOU ROUGE
Pork Chops with Red Cabbage
Serves 4

2 tablespoons bacon drippings
4 large pork chops
Salt
Black pepper
1 medium head red cabbage
2 tart apples
1 onion
1 clove garlic
Pinch of thyme
2 tablespoons vinegar
2 tablespoons sugar

Heat drippings in heavy skillet or pot that has tight-fitting lid. Brown chops on both sides; season with salt and pepper; remove from skillet. Cut cabbage into fourths and slice in processor using slicing disc. Put cabbage in colander, place under running water; drain slightly. Cut apples in half and core (do not peel); cut onion in half. Slice apples and onion in processor using slicing disc; remove to bowl. Put garlic in processor using steel blade; process until minced. Add cabbage to hot fat in pan pork was browned in; quickly cover with lid. After 3 or 4 minutes add apples, onion, garlic, thyme, vinegar and sugar. Cover and barely boil for 1 hour, stirring occasionally. Add a little water if mixture is too dry. Place pork chops on top and cook 30 minutes longer.

PÂTÉ À LA COLMER
Colmer's Pork Loaf
Serves 6

1/4 clove garlic
1 shallot
3/4 pound lean pork
1/4 pound pork fat
1/2 pound pork liver
2 eggs
1 tablespoon flour
1 tablespoon brandy
1 teaspoon salt
1/2 teaspoon black pepper
1/4 cup dry white wine
Pinch of thyme
1/2 teaspoon allspice
4 slices bacon

Put garlic and shallot in processor using steel blade; process until finely chopped. Cut lean pork and pork fat into cubes 2 or 3 inches square. Add to shallot in processor and process until coarsely ground. Remove to bowl. Cut liver into strips or chunks; put in processor. Process until coarsely ground. Add eggs, flour, brandy, salt, pepper, wine, thyme and allspice. Process a few seconds longer until ingredients are blended. Add liver mixture to pork; stir together. Mixture will be very liquid. Line a 9- or 10-inch metal loaf pan with bacon; add pork mixture. Cover top with aluminum foil. Make a slit in top of foil; roll a small strip of foil around a wooden spoon handle, remove and insert in slit. This is a chimney for steam to escape. Set pan in a larger pan of hot water so that water comes half-way up side of pan. Bake in 350° oven 2 hours. Remove pan from water bath and cool slightly before unmolding.

PÀTÉ CHAUD BOURGEOIS
Pork, Chicken, Wine and Liver in Pastry
Serves 8 to 10

This pâté is a combination of pork, chicken and liver, well seasoned and baked in pastry. Very pretty, very French.

Pâté à Foncer (Pastry) Make 2 batches:
1-1/2 cups plus 2 tablespoons flour
Dash of salt
6 tablespoons butter, frozen
2 tablespoons shortening, frozen
1 egg
2 teaspoons heavy cream
3 to 4 tablespoons cold water

Place flour and salt in processor using steel blade. Cut butter into 1-inch pieces; add along with shortening. Process until butter is cut into pieces about the size of small peas. Combine egg, cream and 3 tablespoons water. With processor on add egg mixture. The dough should become damp enough to form into a ball. If it looks too dry add more water, about 1/2 teaspoon at a time. As soon as ball forms, stop processor; do not overmix. Remove dough. Make a second recipe of dough. Combine balls into one big ball; wrap in wax paper and chill in refrigerator 2 hours.

Pâté (Meat Filling)
1 pound lean pork
1 chicken breast
4 chicken thighs
3/4 cup Madeira
3 ounces salt pork
5 chicken livers
2 tablespoons butter
2 eggs
1 tablespoon heavy cream
1-1/2 teaspoons salt
Dash of black pepper
3 ounces pâté de foie gras or liver pâté
1 truffle, optional
1 egg yolk, beaten

Cut pork into cubes about 2 inches by 2 inches or smaller. Put in processor using steel blade. Process until ground. Transfer to bowl. Skin and debone chicken parts. Cut breast meat lengthwise into slices. Add slices to pork, pour Madeira over all; cover and refrigerate 4 to 6 hours. Chop chicken thigh meat into 1/2-inch cubes; cover and refrigerate until needed. Cut rind from salt pork; slice thinly. Cover salt pork with water and simmer 10 minutes; drain. "Sweat" chicken livers by cooking, covered, in butter over very low heat 5 to 8 minutes or until juices and moisture appear (do not brown); chop. Remove chicken breast strips from marinade. Add chopped chicken thigh meat and livers, eggs, cream, salt and pepper to pork and marinade. Mix well.

To Assemble Pâté

Roll out chilled pastry into a rectangle large enough to fit a 2-quart rectangular mold and to cover the top after filling is added. Fit into mold. Distribute slices of salt pork on pastry. Add half of the pork mixture, cover with chicken breast strips and press down lightly. Spread the liver pâté over chicken. Slice truffle very thinly and arrange in center along the length of the pâté. Cover with remaining pork mixture. Fold the overlapping pastry to cover, moisten the edges with water and seal, pressing firmly with the fingers. Make two 1/2-inch holes in top crust. Slip 2-inch-long tubes of foil in each to act as chimneys for escaping steam. Brush top with beaten egg yolk and decorate the surface with crisscrossing lines made with the point of a sharp knife. Bake in 350° oven 1 hour. Cover with foil if pastry begins to brown too quickly. Cool at least 10 minutes before serving. Cut into slices.

Vegetables

Végétaux

PURÉE DE FLAGEOLETS
Lima Bean Purée
Serves 3 to 4

Lima bean purée is thick enough to stay in a mound when served. Delicately flavored with onion and a few drops of lemon juice, it goes well with chicken and pork.

2 pounds fresh lima beans or 1 pound frozen beans
1/2 medium onion
1 cup boiling water
2 tablespoons butter
Salt to taste
Black pepper to taste
Squeeze of lemon juice

Shell beans. Cut onion in half and put in processor using steel blade. Process until coarsely chopped. Add beans and onion to water in saucepan. Cover and cook 15 to 20 minutes or until beans are tender. Drain, reserving liquid. Put beans and onion in processor using steel blade. Process until puréed. If mixture seems too dry add several tablespoons cooking liquid. Melt butter in saucepan. Add purée and salt and pepper. Stir constantly while heating. Mixture should be moist enough to fall from spoon. If too thick add more cooking liquid. Add a few drops lemon juice.

BROCOLI EN PURÉE
Puréed Broccoli
Serves 6

2 pounds fresh broccoli
1 tablespoon salt
3 quarts boiling water
4 tablespoons butter
Dash of black pepper
1 egg, hard cooked

Cut broccoli flowerets from stems. Peel stems carefully with vegetable peeler. Cut into 2- or 3-inch lengths. Wash stems and flowerets. Add stems and salt to water; boil, uncovered, 5 minutes. Add flowerets and boil 5 minutes longer or until stems are tender when pierced with knife. Drain and put in processor using steel blade. Process until coarsely chopped. Melt butter in saucepan, add broccoli and pepper. Taste and add more salt if necessary. Heat and stir constantly until very hot. Mixture should be soft but firm enough to hold its shape when served on plate. If too dry add some of water broccoli was cooked in. Spoon into serving dish. Peel egg, cut in half, put in processor using steel blade. Process until finely chopped. Sprinkle egg over broccoli.

PURÉE DE HARICOTS VERTS
Green Bean Purée
Serves 3 to 4

1 pound green beans
1 teaspoon salt
3 quarts boiling water
2 tablespoons butter
Dash of black pepper

Wash beans and remove ends; cut into 2-inch lengths. Add beans and salt to water. Cook until barely tender, 15 to 20 minutes. Drain immediately in colander and rinse with cold water to stop cooking. Put beans in processor using steel blade. Process until coarsely puréed. Melt butter in saucepan, add purée and pepper. Taste and adjust seasoning. Heat, stirring constantly, until very hot. Purée should be soft enough to fall from the spoon. If too thick add a few tablespoons hot water or water beans were cooked in. Serve immediately.

HARICOTS VERTS
Green Beans and Onions
Serves 4

1 pound green beans
1/2 teaspoon salt
2 quarts boiling water
1 medium onion
2 tablespoons butter
1/4 teaspoon salt
Dash of black pepper
4 or 5 sprigs parsley

Wash beans and cut off ends. Add beans and salt to boiling water. Boil 8 to 10 minutes or until barely done but still crunchy; drain, rinse with cold water to stop cooking process. Spread on paper towels to dry. Cut onion in half; slice in processor using slicing disc. Heat butter in skillet; add onions and sauté 5 to 6 minutes. Add beans, salt and pepper. Sauté and stir until beans are lightly browned. Mince parsley in processor using steel blade. Add parsley to beans, mix well.

PETITS POIS À LA FRANÇAISE
Tiny Peas and Lettuce
Serves 6

1 head iceberg lettuce
2 pounds fresh green peas or 2 10-ounce
    packages frozen green peas
4 tablespoons butter
2 sprigs fresh thyme or 1/2 teaspoon dry thyme
4 sprigs parsley
1/2 teaspoon salt
Dash of black pepper

Cut lettuce into eighths and slice in processor using slicing disc. Shell peas. Melt butter in saucepan, add lettuce, peas and remaining ingredients. Cover and barely simmer until peas are tender, about 20 to 30 minutes for fresh peas; 15 to 20 minutes for frozen peas. Stir occasionally and if necessary add a small amount of water. Moisture from lettuce should be sufficient. Remove thyme and parsley sprigs before serving.

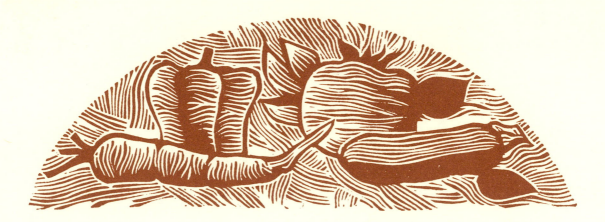

CHOUX VERTS
Green Cabbage
Serves 4 to 5

1 head of cabbage, about 2 pounds
1/2 teaspoon salt
3 quarts boiling water
4 tablespoons melted butter
Dash of black pepper
3 or 4 sprigs parsley

Remove any limp or damaged outer leaves from cabbage. Wash cabbage, drain and cut into eighths. Slice in processor using slicing disc. Add cabbage and salt to boiling water. Bring back to boil and cook 5 to 8 minutes or until tender. Drain, toss with butter and pepper. Chop parsley in processor using steel blade. Spoon cabbage into serving dish; sprinkle parsley on top.

CAROTTES VICHY
Glazed Carrots
Serves 4

1 pound carrots
1/2 teaspoon salt
2 tablespoons butter
1 teaspoon sugar
4 sprigs parsley

Scrape carrots, slice in processor using slicing disc. Put carrots and salt in saucepan; add water to cover. Simmer, uncovered, 15 to 20 minutes or until just tender. Drain off water, add butter and sugar; return to heat. Lightly turn carrots in pan to coat with butter. Put parsley sprigs in processor using steel blade; process until minced. Add parsley to carrots; toss.

PAIN DE CAROTTES
Carrot Loaf
Serves 4 to 5

This vegetable dish is prepared and served like a soufflé, but is made with only two eggs.

1 pound carrots
3/4 teaspoon salt
1 medium onion
4 tablespoons butter
2 tablespoons flour
1 cup half-and-half cream
Black pepper to taste
Pinch of nutmeg
2 tablespoons Madeira
2 eggs, separated

Scrape carrots, slice in processor using slicing disc. Put carrots and 1/2 teaspoon of the salt in saucepan; add water to cover. Bring to boil, reduce heat and simmer uncovered 10 to 15 minutes or until carrots are tender. Drain; put in processor using steel blade. Process until puréed; transfer to bowl. Cut onion in fourths; put in processor using steel blade. Process until finely chopped. Combine onion and butter in saucepan; cook on medium heat 5 to 6 minutes. Add flour and stir until smooth; continue stirring and gradually add cream. Cook on medium heat, stirring constantly, until thick. Add remaining salt, pepper, nutmeg and Madeira. Beat egg yolks slightly; add several spoonfuls of hot sauce. Add egg mixture to sauce, stirring constantly. Then add carrot purée. Beat egg whites until stiff, fold into carrot mixture. Pour into buttered 4-cup soufflé dish or casserole. Bake in 350° oven 30 to 35 minutes.

AUBERGINES FARCIES
Stuffed Eggplant
Serves 4

2 Japanese eggplants (long and slender variety)
2 tablespoons vegetable oil
1 medium onion
1 clove garlic
1/4 pound mushrooms
4 tablespoons butter
1 tablespoon olive oil
2 tablespoons flour
1 cup half-and-half cream
1/2 teaspoon salt
Dash of black pepper
Dash of nutmeg
1 tablespoon Madeira, optional
2 tablespoons fine bread crumbs, see Basics

Cut eggplants in half lengthwise. Make deep crosswise slashes through the meat of each eggplant, being careful not to pierce skin. Heat vegetable oil in skillet. Place cut side of eggplant down in skillet; sauté about 10 minutes; turn and cook skin side about 5 minutes. Cook until meat is tender. Remove meat from skin, being careful to leave skin intact.

Cut onion into fourths, put in processor using steel blade. Process until coarsely chopped; remove. Put garlic in processor using steel blade. Process until minced. With garlic in processor, add mushrooms. Process until mushrooms are coarsely chopped. Melt 2 tablespoons of the butter and the olive oil in heavy saucepan; add onion, garlic and mushrooms. Sauté for 5 minutes. Stir in flour and cook 2 minutes. Add cream, salt, pepper, nutmeg and Madeira. Stir constantly and cook until thick.

Put eggplant meat in processor using steel blade; process until smooth. Add sauce. Process until blended. Fill eggplant skin. Sprinkle with crumbs. Dot with remaining 2 tablespoons butter. Bake in 400° oven 20 minutes.

POMMES DE TERRE AUX HERBES
Herbed Potatoes
Serves 8

2 pounds potatoes
4 egg yolks
1/4 pound butter
1 teaspoon tarragon
1 teaspoon chervil
1/2 teaspoon salt
Dash of black pepper
Dash of nutmeg
1/2 to 2/3 cup flour

Peel potatoes, boil in salted water to cover till tender. Drain, spread on baking sheet and put in 325° oven for 10 minutes to dry. Put in processor using steel blade. Process until smooth. Add egg yolks, half the butter, half the herbs and season with salt, pepper and nutmeg. Spread about half the flour on a board and knead the potato mixture until smooth. Refrigerate until firm.

Butter outside bottom of two 8- or 9-inch cake pans or a baking sheet. Divide potato mixture into 2 portions. Use as much flour as necessary to roll each piece into an 8- or 9-inch circle 1/3 inch thick. Lay circle on bottom of inverted cake pans; trim off excess dough. Or, trim each in a neat circle and lay on a baking sheet. Prick in several places. Heat remaining butter to nut brown, brush over top of potatoes. Bake in 375° oven 20 minutes or until brown. Brush top with butter, sprinkle with remaining herbs. Slice into wedges.

RISOTTE AUX ÉPINARDS
Rice and Spinach
Serves 8

1/2 small onion
6 tablespoons butter
1-1/2 cups uncooked rice
3 cups boiling water
2 teaspoons salt
1 pound fresh spinach
2 quarts boiling water

Cut onion in half, put in processor using steel blade; process until finely chopped. Melt 4 tablespoons of the butter in heavy skillet or casserole; add onion and cook 5 to 6 minutes or until onion is tender. Add rice; use moderate heat and stir frequently until rice grains become translucent and then milky in color. Do not brown rice. Add 3 cups boiling water and 1-1/2 teaspoons of the salt. Cover and simmer 18 to 20 minutes or until all liquid is absorbed and rice is barely tender.

Meanwhile, remove stems of spinach at base of leaf. If spinach is rather large and mature remove more stem by cutting it out with a knife. Wash thoroughly; drop into 2 quarts boiling water. Add remaining 1/2 teaspoon salt; boil slowly about 5 minutes. Taste for doneness. Drain thoroughly in colander, press with spoon to remove more moisture. Put spinach in processor using steel blade, process a few seconds to coarsely chop. Combine spinach, rice and remaining 2 tablespoons butter; toss lightly but thoroughly. Pack into well-buttered 5-cup mold. Cover with wax paper. Set in pan of boiling water (1 to 2 inches deep); bake in 300° oven for 10 minutes. Unmold on serving platter.

RIZ PILAF
Rice Pilaf
Serves 6

1 medium onion
1 tablespoon butter
1 tablespoon vegetable oil
1-1/2 cups uncooked rice
2 cups chicken stock, see Basics
1 cup water
1-1/2 teaspoons salt

Cut onion into fourths. Put in processor using steel blade; process until coarsely chopped. Heat butter and oil in skillet or 2-quart casserole; add onion and sauté 5 minutes. Add rice; stir and cook until grains become translucent and then milky in color. Do not brown rice. Add chicken stock, water and salt. Bring to boil, cover, reduce heat and barely simmer 15 minutes or until rice is tender. Toss lightly with fork.

Note If canned chicken stock is used, omit salt.

SALADE DE CONCOMBRES
Cucumber Salad
Serves 4 to 6

3 to 4 cucumbers
Salt
1/2 cup crème fraîche, see Basics
Dash of white pepper
6 leaves mint
6 sprigs parsley

Peel cucumbers. If they are very mature remove seeds by cutting them in half lengthwise and removing the seeds with a spoon. If cucumbers are young this step is not necessary. Slice cucumbers in processor using slicing disc. Sprinkle with salt and let stand in colander 30 minutes. Combine with crème fraîche and pepper; chill. Put mint leaves and parsley in processor using steel blade. Process until minced. When ready to serve, sprinkle mint and parsley over cucumbers and toss.

Breads and Desserts
Pains et Desserts

PÂTÉ A BRIOCHE
Rich Yeast Bread
Makes 1 loaf

1 tablespoon sugar
2 tablespoons hot water
1/2 package dry yeast (1-1/4 teaspoons)
2 tablespoons milk
2 eggs
4 tablespoons melted butter, cooled
3/4 teaspoon salt
2 cups less 2 tablespoons flour

Egg Glaze
1 egg
1 teaspoon water

Dissolve sugar in hot water, let cool to lukewarm. Sprinkle yeast over top and let stand 10 minutes. Put milk, eggs, butter and salt in processor using steel blade. Add yeast mixture and process for a few seconds. With processor on quickly add 1-3/4 cups of flour through feed tube. If batter does not form a ball immediately add remaining 2 tablespoons flour. (If dough does not form a ball immediately the dough may get under blade and lift it from bottom of bowl. If this happens, turn processor off and remove dough from bowl, reseat blade, add dough and the additional 2 tablespoons flour. Process 20 to 30 seconds longer.)

Generously butter or oil a 3-quart bowl. Place dough in bowl; brush top with oil. Cover bowl with towel and set in barely warm place (75°) until dough has tripled in bulk, about 1-1/2 hours. Punch dough down and form into desired shape.

Butter the interior of a brioche pan which measures about 3-1/2 inches at base of pan. Cut off about three quarters of dough; with lightly floured hands knead lightly and form into a ball. Place in bottom of pan. Make a funnel-shaped hole in the center of the dough 2-1/2 inches deep. Roll the remaining dough between lightly floured palms of your hands to make a ball, then a teardrop shape. Insert pointed end of teardrop into the hole. Set aside, uncovered and free from drafts, in an area with a temperature of around 75° until dough is doubled in bulk (about 1 hour). Just before baking beat together egg and water. Paint surface with egg glaze, being sure not to glaze where the head joins the main body of the brioche. After a moment, glaze with second coat. Bake in 400° oven 15 minutes. Reduce heat to 350° and bake 20 to 25 minutes longer. Cool on a rack 15 to 20 minutes before serving.

Individual Brioches
Dough may be baked in individual brioche pans. Butter pans and shape dough as for large brioche. Let dough rise in a warm place (about 75°) until doubled in bulk (about 30 minutes). Coat twice with egg glaze. Bake in 400° oven 15 to 20 minutes. Makes 12 to 14 rolls.

Note Brioche dough may also be baked in a conventional bread pan, although it is less traditionally French to do so.

CROISSANTS
Crescent Rolls
Makes 12

1 package dry yeast (1 scant tablespoon)
1/4 cup warm water
1 tablespoon sugar
3/4 cup milk
2-1/2 cups flour
1/4 teaspoon salt
1/4 pound butter
Additional flour
1 egg
1 teaspoon water

Stir yeast, water and sugar together. Heat milk to lukewarm (110°) and add it to yeast mixture. Put flour and salt in processor using steel blade. Cut 1 tablespoon of the butter into three pieces and add to processor. Process for a few seconds to cut butter into flour. With processor on add yeast-milk mixture. Dough should be fairly moist; if necessary add an additional tablespoon of milk. Process 10 to 15 seconds longer to knead. Chill 15 minutes.

Lightly flour the remaining butter. Put between two sheets of wax paper; flatten by pounding with rolling pin. Fold butter, again place between two sheets of wax paper; flatten by pounding (use more flour if butter becomes sticky) until pliable but not sticky. Shape butter into a 5-inch square and flour lightly. Turn dough out onto a floured formica or marble counter. Pat dough with flour and roll in a 12-inch square, leaving a hump of dough in center. To do this, start rolling about 2 inches from center of dough and roll toward edge. Do not roll all the way across the square. Set butter in center of dough and fold dough over it like an envelope. Wrap in plastic wrap and chill 15 minutes.

Put chilled dough back on floured work surface, flap side up; bring rolling pin down on dough three to four times to flatten slightly. Roll dough out into a rectangle 5 to 6 inches wide and 14 to 15 inches long. Fold the top third of dough down over the center third; then fold up the bottom third of dough (like a letter). Seal edges by pressing with rolling pin and give the dough a quarter turn to bring open ends to top and bottom. Repeat, rolling dough into a 5 by 14-inch rectangle, folding in thirds, and sealing open ends. Keep a record of these "turns" by marking the dough lightly with the appropriate number of fingerprints (two prints at this point). Wrap dough in plastic, chill 15 minutes.

Repeat the rolling and folding process, giving the dough six turns all together, with a 15-minute rest in the refrigerator between every two turns. Cover and chill at least 1 hour or up to 2 days before using.

Lightly butter two baking sheets. Remove chilled dough and cut in half crosswise. Return one half to refrigerator. Roll other half into a 5 by 14-inch rectangle. If dough seems to be too soft, stop and chill longer. Cut dough obliquely across width to make six triangles 5 inches high. Separate triangles and roll up each triangle from its wide end toward the point of the triangle. Bend ends to make a crescent shape. Place on baking sheet with point of triangle on bottom. Repeat with remaining dough. Let croissants rise in a barely warm place (75°) for 30 to 40 minutes or until almost double in size. Beat together the egg and water; brush croissants with egg glaze. Bake in 425° oven 10 to 12 minutes or until golden brown. Best served while hot.

GATEAU SIMPLE AU CHOCOLAT
Simple Chocolate Cake
Serves 6

This cake is appropriately named. It is simple to make but rich and very good.

4 ounces (squares) sweet dark chocolate
1/4 pound butter
2 cups confectioners' sugar
2 egg yolks
1/2 teaspoon vanilla extract
3 tablespoons brandy or sweetened strong coffee
    and rum (see note)
8 ladyfingers, split
Chocolate Butter Cream, page 93

Break chocolate into pieces, put in a heatproof bowl and set bowl over a pan of hot, but not boiling, water. Stir frequently until chocolate melts. Remove bowl from water bath and let cool to room temperature. Soften butter at room temperature. Place butter, sugar and egg yolks in processor using plastic blade. Process until thoroughly blended. Add cooled chocolate and vanilla; process until blended. Pour brandy or coffee-rum mixture into a shallow bowl or saucer. Dip ladyfinger halves into liquid in saucer, barely touching surface. Arrange a row of four halves side by side on serving dish. Spoon about 1-1/2-inch layer of Chocolate Butter Cream over. Continue making layers, finishing with chocolate cream on top and sides. Dip a spatula in hot water, smooth sides and top of cake. Cover loosely with plastic wrap. Refrigerate 4 hours or overnight.

Note For a coffee-rum dipping liquid, sweeten 1/4 cup strong coffee to suit your taste; stir in 1 tablespoon rum.

AMANDINE AU CHOCOLAT
Chocolate Almond Cake
Serves 8

This chocolate spongecake is made in one layer, cut in half horizontally and filled with a chocolate butter cream.

3 ounces (squares) semisweet chocolate
2 tablespoons rum or coffee
3 eggs, separated
1/8 teaspoon cream of tartar
Pinch of salt
1 tablespoon sugar
1/4 cup toasted blanched almonds
2/3 cup sugar
6 tablespoons butter
1/4 teaspoon almond extract
2/3 cup flour

Chocolate Butter Cream
2 ounces (squares) semisweet chocolate
3 egg yolks
6 tablespoons sugar
1 tablespoon water
9 tablespoons softened butter
1 tablespoon rum

Confectioners' sugar

Combine chocolate and rum, set over hot water until chocolate melts. Cool until barely warm.

Combine egg whites and cream of tartar; beat until egg whites hold soft peaks; continue beating, adding salt and 1 tablespoon sugar, until stiff. Set aside. Turn on processor using steel blade; add almonds through feed tube. Process until ground; remove. Put egg yolks in processor using steel blade. With processor on add almonds and remaining ingredients in order listed. Add chocolate-rum mixture. Transfer to large bowl; add about one quarter of the beaten egg whites, fold in (this lightens batter). Add remaining egg whites and fold in. Lightly butter bottom and sides of an 8- or 9-inch cake pan; add flour and shake to coat; invert to remove excess flour. Pour in batter and bake in 325° oven 25 to 30 minutes or until done. Let cool in pan 10 minutes. Run a thin knife around cake to free from pan; turn out on rack. Cool 2 hours.

While cake cools, make Chocolate Butter Cream. Break chocolate into pieces, put in heatproof bowl and set bowl over a pan of hot, not boiling, water. Stir frequently until chocolate melts. Remove bowl from water bath and let chocolate cool to room temperature. Put egg yolks in processor. Combine sugar and water in saucepan, bring to boil, shake pan frequently and boil until sugar reaches soft ball stage (236° to 238° on candy thermometer). Turn processor on, add sugar mixture slowly. Add butter, rum and melted chocolate; blend. Chill thoroughly.

When cake is cooled and chocolate cream is cold, cut cake in half horizontally. Spread cream on lower layer, replace top layer. Sprinkle top generously with confectioners' sugar.

GATEAU BASQUE
Basque Cake
Serves 4

1/4 cup toasted blanched almonds
6 tablespoons butter
2 tablespoons shortening
1-1/2 cups flour
Pinch of salt
1/4 cup sugar
1 egg yolk
1/2 teaspoon almond extract
3 tablespoons cold water
1/2 to 3/4 cup plum jam
1 egg white, lightly beaten
Additional sugar for dusting

Turn on processor using steel blade; add almonds through feed tube. Process until finely ground; remove and set aside. Put butter and shortening in processor using steel blade. Process until well blended. Add flour, salt, sugar and ground almonds. In a small bowl, combine egg yolk, almond extract and cold water. Start processor and add yolk mixture through feed tube. Mixture should form into a ball; wrap in wax paper; chill 1 hour.

Roll out two thirds of dough on a lightly floured cloth. Roll into a circle about 9 inches in diameter. Use cake pan for pattern, place on pastry and cut out circle. Carefully fold in half and transfer circle to ungreased baking sheet; unfold. Measure jam into a bowl, mix thoroughly with fork, spread evenly on circle leaving a 1/2-inch edge free of jam. Roll remaining pastry into a 9-inch circle; trim. Moisten edge of bottom circle with water; top with remaining circle, seal edges by pressing down with tines of fork. Mark the top in cartwheel fashion with the point of a knife, cutting through to the layer of jam. Bake in 400° oven for 15 minutes or until lightly brown. Have egg white and sugar ready when you remove cake from oven. Brush top with egg white, sprinkle with sugar, return to oven for 3 minutes. Cool slightly and slide onto cooling rack. May be served hot or cool.

ORANGES MERVEILLES
Butter Spongecake
Serves 8

French cakes usually contain no leavening ingredients such as baking powder or soda. Their lightness is the result of folding beaten whites into the batter.

Spongecake
4 eggs, separated
1/8 teaspoon cream of tartar
Pinch of salt
2/3 cup plus 2 tablespoons sugar
1 teaspoon vanilla extract
1 cup flour
5 tablespoons melted butter

Butter Cream
2 egg yolks
1 cup confectioners' sugar
2 tablespoons orange liqueur or 1 teaspoon
    vanilla extract
12 tablespoons butter

Apricot Glaze
3/4 cup apricot preserves
2 tablespoons sugar

1 cup toasted blanched almonds

To make cake, combine egg whites and cream of tartar; beat until soft peaks form. Add salt and 2 tablespoons sugar and continue beating until stiff. Set aside. Put egg yolks in processor using steel blade. With processor on add 2/3 cup sugar and remaining cake ingredients in order listed. Transfer batter to large bowl. Add small portion of egg whites and fold in. Add remaining whites and fold in. Generously butter bottom and sides of a 9- or 10-inch cake pan; add a few spoonfuls of flour and shake to coat bottom and sides. Invert to remove excess flour. Pour batter into prepared pan; bake in 350° oven 25 to 30 minutes. Let cool in pan 10 minutes. Run a thin knife around cake to free from pan; turn out on cooling rack. Cool 2 hours.

While cake cools, prepare Butter Cream. Put egg yolks in processor using steel blade. With processor on add sugar and liqueur or vanilla. Then add the butter 1 or 2 tablespoons at a time. Chill until firm.

Just before assembling cake, make Apricot Glaze. Heat preserves, strain, return to saucepan. Add sugar and boil 1 to 2 minutes or until thick enough to coat spoon. Turn on processor using steel blade; add almonds through feed tube. Process until ground; remove. Cut cake in half horizontally; spread Butter Cream on lower layer, replace top layer. Brush warm glaze on top and sides of cake. Press almonds against side of cake. All the almonds will not adhere but use as many as you can. Save remaining almonds for future use. Store in refrigerator.

DACQUAISE
Meringue Cake
Serves 8

1 cup toasted blanched almonds
2 tablespoons sugar
2 tablespoons cornstarch
1/4 cup unsweetened cocoa powder
6 egg whites
1/2 cup sugar

Butter Cream
2 egg yolks
1 cup plus 2 tablespoons confectioners' sugar
1/2 cup milk, heated
1/2 cup unsweetened cocoa powder
1/2 pound butter

Additional confectioners' sugar

Turn processor on using steel blade and add almonds through feed tube. Process until finely ground, turn off. Add 2 tablespoons sugar, the cornstarch and cocoa; process until well blended. In large bowl, beat egg whites until they begin to form soft peaks. Continue to beat and gradually add 1/2 cup sugar. Beat whites until very firm. Using a rubber spatula, fold almond mixture into egg whites. Generously butter the bottoms of the outsides of two 9-inch cake pans; sprinkle lightly with flour. Spread half of meringue mixture on each inverted pan. Bake in 250° oven for 60 to 90 minutes or until it feels dry and crisp. Cool 10 minutes, then slide onto racks to cool completely.

While cake cools, make Butter Cream. Put egg yolks in processor using steel blade. Start processor and add sugar gradually through feed tube. Blend well. Add hot milk and process till blended. Pour entire mixture into saucepan. Cook on medium heat, stirring constantly, until mixture coats spoon. Do not allow custard to boil. Pour into bowl and cool to room temperature. Place cooled custard in processor using steel blade. Turn processor on and add cocoa; then add butter, about 2 tablespoons at a time. Process until all butter is added and mixture is smooth.

When ready to assemble, place one meringue layer on serving dish. Spoon Butter Cream into pastry bag using a large star tube. Pipe rosettes all around edge of layer; continue toward center until entire layer is covered (use most of cream). Gently place second layer on top of rosettes. Sprinkle generously with confectioners' sugar; form a large rosette of cream in center. Serve immediately or chill 1 hour before serving.

BABAS AUX FRUITS
Rum Raisin Cakes
Makes 12

Babas are little cakes leavened with yeast, soaked with rum, brushed with apricot glaze and served with a dollop of whipped cream. They can be frozen plain, then warmed and soaked with syrup and glazed the day you plan to serve them.

1 package dry yeast (1 scant tablespoon)
1/4 teaspoon sugar
2 tablespoons warm water
1-3/4 cups flour
2 tablespoons sugar
1/2 teaspoon salt
2 eggs
4 tablespoons soft butter
2 tablespoons currants
2 tablespoons raisins
3 tablespoons dark rum
Additional flour

Rum Syrup
1-1/2 cups water
1 cup sugar
1/2 cup dark rum

Apricot Glaze
3/4 cup apricot jam
2 tablespoons water
1 tablespoon dark rum

Sliced toasted almonds
1 cup sweetened whipped cream

Sprinkle yeast and 1/4 teaspoon sugar over water; let stand 10 minutes. Put flour, 2 tablespoons sugar, salt, eggs, butter and yeast mixture in processor using steel blade. Process until mixture is blended and forms a ball. Transfer the dough to a lightly buttered or oiled bowl, cover with a damp cloth. Let rise in a warm place for 1 to 1-1/2 hours or until double in bulk.

Soak currants and raisins in rum overnight or while dough is rising. Drain fruits, reserving rum, and pat dry with paper towels; dust with flour and shake in sieve to remove excess flour. Chill 12 baba tins; brush with melted butter and chill again; brush with butter a second time.

Deflate dough with hand or spoon; add fruit and stir in. Use spoon or well-greased hands to divide dough into 12 equal portions; put into tins (tins should be about one-third full). Let dough rise in warm place until it reaches top of tins, about 1 to 1-1/2 hours. Put in center of 400° oven, reduce temperature to 375° and bake 12 to 15 minutes or until well browned. Turn babas out on a rack and let cool 20 minutes. They should still be warm when soaked with rum syrup.

While babas bake and cool, make rum syrup. Bring water and sugar to boil in saucepan, stirring until sugar is completely dissolved and liquid is clear. Remove from heat, add rum; let cool. Prick sides of warm babas at 1-inch intervals with sharp-pronged fork or toothpick. Put babas on rack over a tray or pan to catch drippings; spoon warm syrup over all several times. Pour syrup from tray back into saucepan and continue spooning over babas until they are moist and spongy but still hold their shape. You may serve babas at this stage with whipped cream, if you wish. The more classic presentation is with apricot glaze.

To make glaze, heat jam and water till melted; force through sieve to eliminate bits of fruit and skin. Reheat to boil. Remove from heat; stir in rum. Use pastry brush and brush glaze on top and sides of babas. Garnish with sliced toasted almonds and top with sweetened whipped cream.

Note Muffin tins may be used in place of baba tins. Chill and coat pans with two layers of butter as for baba tins. Pinch off and roll balls of dough that will fill pans about two-thirds full. Proceed as in above recipe. Cooking time will be about the same.

SAVARIN
Rum Cake Ring
Serves 8 to 12

Babas aux Fruits dough, preceding, omitting fruit

Rum Syrup
1 cup water
3/4 cup sugar
3 tablespoons dark rum

Apricot Glaze
1/2 cup apricot jam
1 tablespoon water
1 tablespoon dark rum

Slivered toasted almonds

Prepare yeast dough as directed in recipe; let rise until double in bulk. Do not add rum-soaked fruits. Coat a chilled ring mold (9 to 9-1/2 inches across top, with a 4-inch opening) with melted butter. Punch dough down and form into a cylinder shape long enough to fit in the mold with ends meeting. Press ends together. Brush top lightly with melted butter; set in warm place and let rise until double in bulk. Place in 400° oven 10 minutes; reduce heat to 350° and bake 15 to 20 minutes longer or until well browned. Oil wires of cake rack, invert cake on rack. Let cool 20 minutes; cake should be warm when soaked with rum syrup.

While cake bakes, prepare syrup. Combine water and sugar in saucepan. Bring to boil and stir until sugar is completely dissolved and liquid is clear. Remove from heat, add rum and cool to lukewarm. Set rack with warm cake over a tray or pan to catch drippings; spoon syrup over cake. Pour syrup from tray back into saucepan; continue spooning syrup over cake until cake is moist and spongy but still holds its shape. Let cake cool, then carefully slide onto serving plate.

To make glaze, heat jam and water to boil; force through sieve to eliminate bits of fruit. Stir in rum. Use a pastry brush and brush glaze on top and sides of cake. Sprinkle almonds over all. Cake may be served plain; or fill center with Crème Saint-Honoré or sweetened whipped cream.

Crème Saint-Honoré (Custard Filling)
10 tablespoons sugar
1/2 cup flour
1/4 teaspoon salt
5 egg yolks
2 cups milk
1 2-inch piece vanilla bean or 1 teaspoon
      vanilla extract
1 envelope unflavored gelatin
1/4 cup cold water
1/4 cup crème fraîche (see Basics) or
      whipped cream
3 egg whites
1/2 cup sugar

Put sugar, flour and salt in saucepan. Stir together with a whisk. Add yolks and just enough of the milk to make a paste. Add remaining milk and vanilla bean, if using. Cook over low heat until thick, stirring constantly. (If you have one, use a spoon with a flat edge at the end so that it will contact more area at bottom of pan.) Remove from heat; discard vanilla bean or add vanilla extract if bean was not used. Soak gelatin in cold water; when moistened add to hot sauce and stir until completely dissolved. Stir in crème fraîche or whipped cream. Set in cold water and stir frequently until cool. Add a dash of salt to egg whites and whip. When whites start to stiffen, gradually add remaining 1/2 cup sugar and beat until very stiff. Fold into cooled sauce. Spoon custard into center of Savarin. Makes about 4 cups of filling.

Note Crème Saint-Honoré may also be used to fill cream puffs, eclairs and tart shells.

PROFITEROLES
Miniature Cream Puffs
Serves 12 to 14

These miniature cream puffs, filled with custard and floating in chocolate syrup, make a beautiful dessert. Serve them in a large glass bowl and let each person serve himself.

Pâté à Choux Sucrée (Dessert Puff Shells)
1 cup water
6 tablespoons butter
1/8 teaspoon salt
2 teaspoons sugar
1 cup flour
3 large eggs
1 additional egg
1/2 teaspoon water

Put water, butter, salt and sugar in heavy saucepan. Bring mixture to boil; boil until butter melts. Remove from heat, add flour all at once and beat vigorously to blend flour. Return to moderate heat; stir and cook for several minutes. Pastry will clean itself off sides and bottom of pan. Keep heating and beating 2 to 3 minutes longer, thus evaporating excess moisture. Remove from heat, spoon into processor using steel blade. With processor on add 3 eggs through feed tube, one at a time. Be sure each egg is mixed in thoroughly before adding the next. Pastry should be stiff

enough to hold its shape when lifted in a spoon. Use immediately or keep warm over hot water for a short time.

To make miniature cream puffs, use a pastry bag and metal tube with opening 1/4 to 1/2 inch in diameter. Fill bag with paste. If you have two ovens, preheat both to 400°. Generously butter two baking sheets; squeeze the paste onto the baking sheets, making mounds slightly larger than chocolate kisses. Combine the additional egg with water; dip pastry brush into beaten egg and slightly flatten each puff using side of brush. (Avoid dripping egg glaze down puff onto baking sheet.) Bake sheets in separate ovens for about 15 to 20 minutes. Puffs will double in size and be firm and crusty to the touch. For this dessert they should be only lightly browned. Remove from oven, turn off heat; pierce each puff with sharp knife. Return to cooled oven for 10 minutes, leaving door ajar. Cool puffs on rack.

If you have only one oven, prepare only one sheet of pastry at a time, keeping other half of pastry over hot water. Glaze and bake as directed. Remove from oven, turn off heat, pierce with knife. Return to oven for 10 minutes, leaving door ajar. Cool puffs. Reheat oven to 400°. Prepare and bake second sheet as you did the first.

Puffs keep well frozen; wrap airtight in plastic. When ready to fill, set frozen puffs in 400° oven 5 minutes. Makes 48 small puffs.

Crème Saint-Honoré (Custard Filling)
5 egg yolks
10 tablespoons sugar
1/4 teaspoon salt
1/2 cup flour
2 cups milk
1 2-inch piece vanilla bean or 1 teaspoon
     vanilla extract
1/4 teaspoon cream of tartar
3 egg whites
6 tablespoons sugar

Put egg yolks in processor using steel blade. With processor on gradually add 10 tablespoons sugar through feed tube. Blend thoroughly. Add salt and flour, mix well. In saucepan combine milk and vanilla bean, if using. Heat to boiling, remove from heat and let stand 10 minutes. Remove bean. (If using vanilla extract, heat milk to boiling, add vanilla. Use immediately.) With processor on add milk through feed tube. Pour mixture into saucepan and cook on moderate heat, stirring constantly until custard boils. Sauce will be lumpy at first, but will smooth out with beating. Reduce heat and cook 2 to 3 minutes after mixture comes to boil. Remove from heat, clean sides of pan with rubber spatula. Dot top with butter to prevent a film from forming; let cool. Add cream of tartar to egg whites and beat until they hold soft peaks. Continue to beat and gradually add remaining 6 tablespoons sugar. Fold into cool custard. Makes about 3 cups of filling.

Sauce au Chocolat (Chocolate Sauce)
8 ounces (squares) semisweet baking chocolate
2 cups water
2 tablespoons butter
2 tablespoons dark rum
2 tablespoons brandy

Break chocolate into pieces. Combine chocolate and water. Let simmer and stir frequently until chocolate is melted and smooth. Add butter, rum and brandy; stir until butter melts. Cool to room temperature before using. Makes 3 cups of sauce.

   When ready to serve, put custard in pastry bag fitted with 1/2-inch metal tube. Fill cream puffs by inserting metal tip of pastry tube into hole earlier pierced in puff with knife. To serve, put puffs in an attractive glass bowl. Add chocolate sauce and serve 3 or 4 puffs to each guest.

CYGNES CHANTILLY
Chantilly Swans
Serves 10 to 12

Chantilly Swans are a delightful party dessert. They are both decorative and delicious.

Pâté à Choux Sucrée for Profiteroles, preceding
1 egg yolk
1/2 teaspoon water

Chantilly (Sweetened Whipped Cream)
1-1/2 cups heavy cream
1-1/2 tablespoons confectioners' sugar
1 teaspoon vanilla extract or 1 tablespoon brandy

Additional confectioners' sugar

Prepare pastry as directed. Put dough into a pastry bag fitted with a 1/2-inch plain tube. On a lightly greased baking sheet pipe at least ten S-shaped lines about 4 to 5 inches in length to form swans' necks. With the rest of the dough, pipe an equal number of ovals, 1 by 3 inches in diameter. Allow several inches between ovals. Beat together egg yolk and water; brush necks and ovals very lightly with egg glaze. (Do not let glaze run down sides onto pan.) Bake in 375° oven 5 to 10 minutes, until necks are golden brown. Remove necks from oven. Reduce oven temperature to 325° and bake ovals 15 to 20 minutes longer or until well browned. Remove ovals to cooling racks; cool 5 to 10 minutes. Slice off tops of ovals and scrape out any soft bits of dough inside. Cut each top piece in half lengthwise to form wings. Necks and bodies may be kept overnight in airtight containers.

To make Chantilly, whip cream until soft peaks form. Continue beating and gradually add sugar. Add vanilla or brandy. Put cream in pastry bag fitted with 1/4-inch star tube. Fill the bottom half of the ovals with cream, insert the neck in one end and angle the two halves of the top piece of pastry to form wings spreading up and out from the base of neck. Sprinkle swans with additional powdered sugar forced through a small sieve. Arrange on serving dishes. Serve immediately.

FLÛTES
Rolled Cookies
Makes 16 to 18

1 egg
1/3 cup sugar
1/4 teaspoon vanilla extract
1/3 cup melted butter, cooled
1/2 cup flour

Put egg in processor using steel blade. With processor on, gradually add sugar through feed tube. Continue mixing and add vanilla, butter and flour. Use a well-buttered or -oiled baking sheet. Make four mounds of batter using slightly rounded teaspoon of batter for each cookie. Spread batter with rubber spatula into a circle 2-1/2 to 3 inches in diameter. Bake in 375° oven 4 to 5 minutes or until batter is cooked but not browned; watch cookies carefully and be ready to roll them. When cooked loosen each cookie with wide spatula, roll around a round handle, perhaps wooden spoon slightly larger than a pencil. Top of flat cookie should be outside of rolled cookie. Press cookie close to handle, then slip off and put on cooling rack. Work fast. If cookies cool they will not roll and must be returned to oven to warm. Repeat with remaining batter.

CRÊPES SUZETTE
Crêpes with Orange Sauce
Serves 6

Crêpes
3/4 cup milk
3/4 cup water
3 eggs
1 tablespoon sugar
2 tablespoons orange liqueur
1-1/2 cups flour
1/3 cup melted butter

Orange Sauce
1/2 pound butter
Grated zest of 1 orange
1-1/2 cups confectioners' sugar
1/4 cup frozen orange juice concentrate, thawed
1/4 cup orange liqueur or Grand Marnier
2 tablespoons sugar
1/3 cup orange liqueur
1/3 cup cognac

Put all ingredients for crepes in processor using steel blade. Process 30 to 60 seconds till well blended. Refrigerate batter 1 to 2 hours. Dip a paper napkin in oil and wipe over bottom of a 6-inch crêpe pan. Heat pan until medium hot, pour in about 2 tablespoons of batter. Tilt pan to cover bottom with batter. Return to heat, cook until batter is dry on top. Turn crêpe using a rubber spatula and your fingers. Leave for a few seconds, then turn out on cooling rack. Repeat with remaining batter, wiping pan with oiled napkin after cooking each crêpe. Do not stack crêpes until completely cool. Makes 16 to 18 6-inch crêpes.

If not used immediately, stack cooled crêpes, wrap in wax paper or plastic wrap and refrigerate. Crêpes will keep in refrigerator 5 to 7 days. They may also be frozen, but must be stacked with wax paper between each crêpe and sealed tightly in a plastic bag. Crêpes will keep in freezer 2 to 3 months.

Prepare sauce just before you plan to serve the crêpes. Put butter in processor using steel blade. Add orange zest, confectioners' sugar, orange juice and liqueur; process until smooth. Heat orange butter in chafing dish until hot. Dip both sides of a crêpe in hot butter; fold in half with the most attractive side of crêpe on the outside; then fold in half again to form a wedge shape. Place at side of pan and repeat with remaining crêpes. Arrange crêpes evenly in pan; sprinkle with 2 tablespoons sugar. In a small saucepan combine orange liqueur and cognac. Heat mixture, pour over crêpes in chafing dish and ignite with match. Spoon sauce over crêpes until flames die down. Serve immediately.

CRÊPES SUCRÉE
Dessert Crêpes
Makes 16 to 18 6-inch crêpes

1 cup milk
1/2 cup half-and-half cream
2 eggs
1 egg yolk
Pinch of salt
1-1/4 cups flour
1 tablespoon sugar
2 tablespoons melted butter

In order listed, put ingredients in processor using steel blade. Process until thoroughly blended. Pour batter into bowl and refrigerate 2 hours before using. Dip a paper napkin in oil and wipe over bottom of a 6-inch crêpe pan. Heat pan until medium hot, pour in about 2 tablespoons of batter. Tilt pan to cover bottom with batter. Return pan to heat, cook until batter is dry on top. Turn crêpe using a rubber spatula and your fingers. Leave for a few seconds, turn out on cooling rack. Repeat with remaining batter, wiping pan with oiled napkin after cooking each crêpe. Do not stack crêpes until completely cool.

If not used immediately, stack cooled crêpes, wrap in wax paper or plastic wrap and refrigerate. Crêpes will keep in refrigerator 5 to 7 days. They may also be frozen, but must be stacked with wax paper between each crêpe and sealed well in a plastic bag. Crêpes will keep in freezer 2 to 3 months.

CRÊPES À LA NORMANDE
Apple Crêpes
Serves 6

3 Winesap apples
1/4 cup sugar
1/2 teaspoon cinnamon
14 Crêpes Sucrée, preceding
1/3 cup melted butter
2 tablespoons firmly packed brown sugar
1/2 cup apple brandy

Peel apples, cut in half and remove core. Slice apples in processor using slicing disc. Combine apples, sugar and cinnamon in saucepan. Cook over low heat for 10 minutes, stirring frequently; cool. Place a tablespoon of apple mixture on each crêpe and carefully roll up. Arrange in buttered baking dish. Drizzle with butter and sprinkle with brown sugar. Bake in 350° oven 15 minutes. Heat brandy in a small pan, pour over crêpes and flame. Serve immediately.

CRÊPES FOURRÉES, FRANGIPANE
Almond Custard Crêpes
Serves 8

Frangipane (Almond Custard Filling)
1/3 cup toasted blanched almonds
1 egg
1 egg yolk
3/4 cup sugar
3 tablespoons flour
1 cup milk, heated
3 tablespoons butter
1/4 teaspoon almond extract
1/4 teaspoon vanilla extract

16 Crêpes Sucrée, page 107
2 ounces (squares) semisweet baking chocolate
2 tablespoons melted butter

Turn on processor using steel blade; add almonds through feed tube and process until almost pulverized. Remove and set aside. Put egg, egg yolk, sugar and flour in processor using steel blade. Process for 20 to 30 seconds; continue processing and gradually add hot milk. Pour all into saucepan, cook on medium heat until thick and rather stiff. Continue to cook 2 to 3 minutes longer. Beat with whisk if custard is lumpy. Add butter, almond and vanilla extracts, and almonds. If not used immediately, clean custard from sides of pan with rubber spatula, then dot top with butter or cover top with plastic wrap. Refrigerate until ready to use. Will keep in refrigerator for a week. Makes about 2 cups of filling.

To fill crêpes, spread a heaping tablespoon of Frangipane on the least attractive side of each crêpe. Fold crêpes into halves, then fourths, or roll them up. Arrange in a flat, buttered baking dish. Grate chocolate over top, then sprinkle with melted butter. Place in 350° oven 8 to 10 minutes or until chocolate melts. Serve hot or warm.

Note If you prefer to flame these crêpes, do not add chocolate and butter. When ready to flame, heat 1/4 cup Grand Marnier, cognac or orange liqueur, pour over crêpes and flame.

CRÊPES FIRENZE
Florentine Crêpes
Serves 6

Crêpes Firenze is my version of the wonderful crêpes served at Harry's Bar in Florence, Italy. It is one of my favorite desserts.

1 cup butter
2 cups confectioners' sugar
1/4 cup Grand Marnier
12 to 14 Crêpes Sucrée, page 107

Put butter, sugar and Grand Marnier in processor using steel blade. Process until well blended. Spread about 1 tablespoon on the least attractive side of each crêpe; fold into fourths. Overlap folded crêpes in a shallow, ovenproof dish. Spread remaining butter mixture on top. When ready to serve, heat in 350° oven 5 to 10 minutes or until butter filling has melted. Serve immediately.

Note To flame dessert, heat 1/4 cup Grand Marnier or orange liqueur, pour over crêpes and ignite.

POMMES BELLE VUE
Apple Mold with Caramel
Serves 8

1 cup sugar
2-1/2 tablespoons water
3 pounds tart apples (about 9 medium)
1/3 cup butter
1/4 teaspoon cinnamon
2 tablespoons fresh lemon juice
4 eggs
1 egg white
1/4 cup rum or orange juice
1 cup sweetened whipped cream

Combine 1/2 cup of the sugar and the water in saucepan. Bring to boil, slowly swirling liquid by rotating pan, until sugar has dissolved completely and liquid is clear. Boil, swirling frequently, until liquid has turned a light brown. Pour into 2-quart mold and turn slowly to coat bottom and sides. Invert pan to drain any excess.

Peel apples; cut in half and remove cores. Slice in processor using slicing disc. Melt butter in large shallow roasting pan. Add apples. Sprinkle remaining 1/2 cup sugar, cinnamon and lemon juice over apples; stir lightly. Cook in 350° oven 15 to 20 minutes or until barely tender. In large mixing bowl combine eggs, egg white and rum or orange juice; fold in apples. Pour into caramelized mold. Set mold in a pan of hot water; bake in 300° oven 50 to 60 minutes or until set in center. Let stand 10 minutes, then unmold. Serve warm or cold with whipped cream.

POMMES MERINGUÉES
Apple Custard with Meringue
Serves 6

2 pounds tart apples (about 6 medium)
3 egg yolks
2 eggs
1/3 cup sugar
1 teaspoon vanilla extract or a 1-inch piece
    vanilla bean
2 cups milk

Meringue
4 egg whites
Dash of cream of tartar
6 tablespoons sugar

Peel, halve and core apples. Slice in processor using slicing disc. Butter a 9-inch-square baking dish; arrange apple slices in dish. Put egg yolks and eggs in processor using steel blade. With processor on add sugar through feed tube. Add vanilla extract, if using. Heat milk to almost boiling, add to processor and blend. (If vanilla bean is used, add to milk, heat till warm and let stand 30 minutes before using. Remove bean, reheat milk until hot and add to egg-sugar mixture; blend.) Pour custard mixture over apple slices. Bake in 300° oven 30 to 35 minutes or until apples are tender and custard is set in center.

While apples are cooking make meringue. Beat egg whites and cream of tartar until stiff. Continue beating and gradually add sugar. Continue beating until sugar is dissolved (test by rubbing mixture between your fingers). Spread meringue on top of apples. Put in 400° oven 8 to 10 minutes or until top is lightly browned.

MONT BLANC
Chestnuts and Whipped Cream
Serves 4 to 5

2 pounds chestnuts
1/2 cup sugar
1 teaspoon vanilla extract
2 cups heavy cream
1/4 cup confectioners' sugar

Make a slit in each chestnut with a sharp knife. Put chestnuts in pressure cooker, using a rack if you have one. Add 3/4 cup water; cook at 15 pounds pressure for 10 minutes. Or place chestnuts in a saucepan, cover with boiling water and boil 25 minutes. Peel chestnuts while still warm by removing thick husk and brown covering. Put nut meats in processor using steel blade. Process until puréed. Continue processing and add sugar and vanilla through feed tube. Mound purée in center of serving dish. Whip cream; fold in confectioners' sugar. Spoon or pipe cream into a "snow cap" making a nice high peak.

PÊCHES MELBA
Peach Melba
Serves 6

Peach Melba is a glamorous-looking dessert. Serve it in large wineglasses, or mold the ice cream in a bowl and unmold into a large glass bowl, rounded side up. Stand peach halves, rounded side out, around ice cream. Drizzle some sauce over all. Serve with additional sauce on side.

6 ripe peaches
1/2 cup sugar
1-1/2 cups water
Few drops red food coloring
1 10-ounce package frozen raspberries
1/2 cup raspberry jelly
1 cup heavy cream
2 to 4 tablespoons confectioners' sugar
1 quart vanilla ice cream

Peel, halve and pit peaches. Combine sugar and water in saucepan; heat. Add peach halves and gently poach until just tender. Add few drops red coloring. Let peaches cool in syrup. Thaw raspberries; put in processor using steel blade. Add jelly and process until mixture is puréed. Remove and set aside. Whip cream; sweeten to taste with powdered sugar.

When ready to serve, spoon ice cream into serving dishes (or unmold as desired). Add two peach halves to each serving and spoon raspberry sauce over all. Top with whipped cream.

TARTE À L'ORANGE
Orange Tart
Serves 8

Pâté Brisée Fine dough, page 16
4 tablespoons apricot preserves
1 teaspoon water

Glazed Oranges
1/4 cup fresh orange juice
1/4 cup fresh lemon juice
1/2 cup sugar
1 large, thick-skinned orange
1/4 cup orange liqueur

Almond Cream Filling
1/4 cup toasted blanched almonds
2 egg yolks
6-1/2 tablespoons sugar
4 tablespoons butter

Prepare pastry and chill as directed in recipe. Roll out dough 2 inches larger than an 8- or 9-inch tart pan with a removable bottom (or use conventional pie pan). Fit dough into pan, trim and crimp edges. Follow directions given in recipe for prebaking pastry. Let cool. Meanwhile heat preserves with water; strain. Coat cool pastry shell with warm preserves.

Combine the juices and sugar; boil 20 minutes. With peel intact, cut the orange horizontally into neat, thin slices. Add to syrup and simmer 10 to 15 minutes longer. Drain slices, reserving syrup, and spread out to dry on rack. When slices are dry, cut into quarters. Return syrup to heat and boil 2 or 3 minutes longer; add orange liqueur. Set aside.

Turn on processor using steel blade; add almonds through feed tube. Process until ground; remove. Put egg yolks in processor using steel blade, process a few seconds. With processor on add sugar, then butter. Add ground almonds. Fill the cooled, coated tart shell with Almond Cream. Bake in 400° oven 8 to 10 minutes or until center is set and golden brown. Cool 10 minutes. Arrange orange slices on top. Pour hot syrup over all. (If syrup has cooled, reheat.) Cool completely before unmolding.

POIRES EN CROÛTE
Pears in Crust
Serves 4

Pâté Brisée Sucrée (Sweet Short Pastry)
2 cups flour
1/2 teaspoon salt
2 tablespoons sugar
1/4 pound butter, frozen
2 tablespoons shortening, frozen
4 to 6 tablespoons cold water

Put flour, salt and sugar in processor using steel blade. Cut butter into 1-inch pieces, add along with shortening. Process until butter is about the size of small peas. With processor on add 3 tablespoons water. Gradually add more water just until mixture forms a ball. Do not process after ball is formed. Wrap in wax paper; chill 1 hour.

4 pears, ripe but firm
1/2 lemon
1 egg
1 teaspoon water

Peel one pear, rub with cut lemon. Divide pastry into four equal parts. Roll one part into a rope about 9 inches long; put on pastry cloth and roll out into rectangle about 9 by 4 inches. Cut a 2-inch circle out of one end. Cut remaining pastry lengthwise into strips 3/4 inch wide. Set pear up-right on circle. Mix together egg and water. Moisten one end of a pastry strip with egg. Start at circle and wind pastry strip around pear, connecting remaining strips as needed by using beaten egg. Wrap pear up to the stem (but do not cover stem); brush entire pastry with egg. Repeat process with 3 remaining pears. Place all sitting upright on well-greased baking sheet. Bake in 400° oven 30 to 35 minutes or until well browned. Serve warm with warm or cold Crème Anglaise.

Crème Anglaise (Thin Custard Sauce)
3 egg yolks
6 tablespoons sugar
1 teaspoon cornstarch
1-1/3 cups milk, heated to scalding
1 teaspoon vanilla extract
1 teaspoon rum

Put egg yolks in processor using steel blade; process. With processor still on add sugar and cornstarch; slowly add hot milk. Pour mixture into saucepan; cook on medium heat, stirring constantly, until sauce thickens just enough to coat spoon (do not let it come near a boil). Take off heat; strain through fine sieve. Add flavoring. Keep sauce over warm water if you want to serve it warm. To serve cold, press plastic wrap directly on top of custard; cool, then chill in refrigerator. Makes about 1-1/2 cups of sauce.

TARTE AUX POMMES
Apple Tart
Serves 6

Pâté Sablée (Short Pastry)
1 cup less 2 tablespoons flour
Pinch of salt
1/4 cup sugar
4 tablespoons butter, frozen
2 egg yolks
1/2 teaspoon vanilla extract

In processor using steel blade, put flour, salt and sugar. Cut butter into 1-inch pieces; add. Process until butter is cut into pieces the size of small peas. With processor on add egg yolks and vanilla; mixture should form a ball. If mixture is too dry add a little water, a teaspoon at a time, until it does form a ball. Do not process after ball is formed. Wrap pastry in wax paper; chill 30 minutes. May be kept in refrigerator 1 to 2 days.

1 cup sugar
2-1/2 pounds Winesap apples (7 or 8 medium)
4 tablespoons butter
2 cups sweetened whipped cream or crème
    fraîche, see Basics

Place 3/4 cup of sugar in heavy 9- or 10-inch ovenproof skillet or flameproof casserole. Heat, stirring occasionally, until melted. Cook to a deep golden caramel color. Immediately set pan in a container of cold water to stop cooking.

Peel, halve and core apples; slice in processor using slicing disc. Arrange one layer of slices in a neat overlapping pattern over the caramel. Dot with a few teaspoons butter and sprinkle with a few teaspoons of remaining sugar. Continue making layers until all apples, butter and sugar are used. Roll chilled pastry and cut into circle to fit inside skillet or casserole and to cover apples. Place pastry over apples. Bake in 375° oven 30 to 35 minutes or until apples are tender and pastry is lightly browned. Invert on a platter with the caramelized side up. Serve warm with sweetened whipped cream or crème fraîche.

TARTE AUX FRAISES
Fresh Strawberry Tart
Serves 8

Pâté Brisée Sucrée, page 115

Prepare pastry as directed in recipe. Roll chilled dough into a 12-inch circle. Fit into a 10-inch quiche pan or conventional pie pan; trim and crimp edge. Butter a large sheet of lightweight aluminum foil and fit in pastry with buttered side down. Fill with dried beans. Bake in 450° oven for 10 to 12 minutes. Remove liner, prick bottom in several places and return to oven. Bake 5 to 10 minutes longer or until brown. Let cool.

Crème Patissière (Custard Filling)
5 egg yolks
10 tablespoons sugar
1/2 cup flour
1/4 teaspoon salt
2 cups milk, heated
1 teaspoon vanilla extract
3 tablespoons butter

Put yolks in processor using steel blade. Start processor and gradually add sugar through feed tube. Blend well. Add flour and salt, then hot milk. Pour entire mixture into a saucepan; cook over medium heat, stirring constantly until thick. Remove from heat and add vanilla and butter; stir till butter melts. Spread plastic wrap on surface to prevent a skin from forming. Chill.

1 cup red currant jelly
2 tablespoons water
1 basket fresh strawberries, capped

When ready to assemble tart, combine jelly and water in a saucepan; bring to boil. Boil until jelly dissolves. Paint inside of pastry shell with some of glaze. Spoon in Crème Patissière; arrange berries on top of custard. Pour remaining glaze over all. Chill 1 hour or more. To serve, cut into wedges.

CHARLOTTE MALAKOFF AU CHOCOLAT
Chocolate Almond Cream
Serves 12

1 cup sugar
1/3 cup water
4 ounces (squares) semisweet chocolate
1/2 cup toasted blanched almonds
1/2 pound butter
1/4 cup dark rum
1/4 teaspoon almond extract
2 cups heavy cream

2 dozen ladyfingers, split
2/3 cup hot water
1/3 cup sugar
3 tablespoons rum
Grated chocolate
Whipped cream, optional

Combine sugar and water in saucepan; stir over heat until sugar has dissolved. Melt chocolate over hot water; add to sugar mixture. Cool mixture until barely warm. Turn on processor using steel blade; add almonds and process until ground. Remove to bowl for later use. Put chocolate mixture in processor using steel blade. With processor on add butter 2 tablespoons at a time; then add rum, almond extract and ground almonds. Remove chocolate mixture to a bowl and refrigerate until cold. Whip cream until stiff; fold into chilled chocolate mixture.

Prepare a 2-quart cylindrical mold, preferably 4 inches deep. Line bottom of mold with round of wax paper. Arrange ladyfingers spoke fashion on wax paper, trimming as necessary to fit closely. Combine water and sugar, stir to dissolve sugar; pour into small flat dish and let cool. Stir in rum and sprinkle several tablespoons over ladyfingers in bottom of mold. Dip remaining ladyfingers into syrup for 1 or 2 seconds, drain on rack. Arrange a row of upright ladyfingers inside the mold, pressed closely together with curved sides against the mold. Reserve remaining ladyfingers for layering in the dessert.

Turn a third of the chocolate mixture into the lined mold, spreading it over the layer of ladyfingers. Arrange another layer of ladyfingers over this, then repeat layers ending with remaining ladyfingers, if any. Trim any ladyfingers protruding above the edge of mold and add trimmings to final layer of ladyfingers. Cover top with wax paper. Find a saucer that fits inside mold, place on top and weight with heavy object. Refrigerate 6 hours or overnight. Butter and chocolate must be chilled firmly so that dessert will hold its shape when unmolded.

To unmold, run long thin knife around inside of mold; turn upside down on serving dish. Decorate with grated or shaved chocolate. Serve plain or with whipped cream.

FLAN PRALINÉE
Praline Custard
Serves 6

1-1/4 cups sugar
2 tablespoons water
2 cups milk
1 3-inch piece vanilla bean or 1 teaspoon
      vanilla extract
3 eggs
3 egg yolks
7 tablespoons praline powder, below
1 cup heavy cream
Confectioners' sugar

In heavy saucepan combine 3/4 cup of the sugar and the water. Heat on medium heat, stirring until sugar dissolves. Continue heating until mixture becomes a light hazelnut brown. Watch constantly. If caramel becomes too brown it will taste burnt. Immediately pour into 4-cup ring mold, tipping mold to coat evenly with caramel. You may have to use a spoon to coat inside of center tube. Syrup will be standing in bottom of mold after sides are coated. Set caramelized mold aside.

In another saucepan heat milk to simmer; add vanilla bean. Remove from heat and let stand 30 minutes; remove bean. If bean is not used, heat milk to scalding (do not boil), add vanilla extract and cool. Put eggs and egg yolks into processor using steel blade. Process and add remaining 1/2 cup sugar through feed tube. With processor still on, add cooled milk. Strain custard mixture through a fine sieve into a bowl. Spoon off any foam. Stir in 3 tablespoons of the praline powder. Pour into caramelized mold. Set mold in pan of hot water. Bake in 325° oven 40 to 45 minutes or until knife inserted in center comes out clean. Remove from oven and water bath; cool. Cover and chill.

To serve, run knife around edge of mold; turn custard out onto serving platter. If any caramel remains in mold add 2 or 3 tablespoons water, heat until caramel dissolves, pour around mold. Whip cream and sweeten to taste with confectioners' sugar; spoon into center of mold. Sprinkle remaining praline powder over cream.

Pralin (Praline Powder)
1 cup toasted blanched almonds
1/2 cup sugar
1 tablespoon water

Lightly grease a baking sheet; spread almonds on sheet in single layer. In heavy saucepan combine sugar and water. Cook over medium heat, stirring until sugar dissolves. Continue to cook until mixture turns a light hazelnut brown. Do not let caramel become dark brown. Pour hot caramel over almonds. When caramel hardens break into small pieces. Turn on processor using steel blade; add caramelized almonds through feed tube. Process until pulverized. Makes about 1-1/2 cups.

Note Fresh fruit may be served in center in place of cream.

SOUFFLÉ AU GRAND MARNIER
Grand Marnier Soufflé
Serves 8 to 10

6 egg yolks
3/4 cup sugar
1/2 cup Grand Marnier
3/4 cup orange juice
2/3 cup flour
1 cup milk
1/2 teaspoon vanilla extract
4 ladyfingers, split
8 egg whites
1 cup heavy cream
2 or 3 tablespoons confectioners' sugar

Put egg yolks in processor using steel blade. With processor on add 1/4 cup sugar through feed tube. Add 1/4 cup Grand Marnier and the orange juice. Add flour and process until blended. Heat milk and 1/4 cup sugar in a 2-quart saucepan; stir until sugar dissolves. Heat to almost boiling; gradually add to egg yolk mixture. Pour all back into saucepan; cook on medium heat, stirring constantly, until very thick. Remove from heat, stir in vanilla. Press wax paper or plastic wrap on top of custard and set pan in cold water to cool. Place ladyfingers in single layer in shallow pan; sprinkle with remaining Grand Marnier.

Prepare soufflé dish. Lightly butter bottom and sides of a 1-1/2-quart soufflé dish fitted with a collar, page 122. Sprinkle evenly with sugar. Beat egg whites until they form soft peaks. Add remaining 1/4 cup sugar and continue beating until stiff peaks form. Gently fold whites into warm custard. Turn half of mixture into prepared soufflé dish. Arrange ladyfingers on top. Pour on remaining mixture. Set dish in pan of hot water; bake in 350° oven 30 to 40 minutes or until golden brown. It should shake lightly; the soft part serves as sauce. Whip cream until stiff; fold in confectioners' sugar to taste. Serve soufflé immediately after removing from oven. Top each portion with whipped cream.

BAVAROIS AU CHOCOLAT
Chocolate Bavarian Cream
Serves 6

1-1/4 cups milk
4 ounces (squares) semisweet chocolate
1 teaspoon unflavored gelatin
1 tablespoon water
4 large egg yolks
5 tablespoons sugar
1/2 teaspoon vanilla extract
2 cups crème fraîche, see Basics
2 tablespoons confectioners' sugar

Heat milk and chocolate in saucepan over low heat; stir frequently until chocolate melts. Combine gelatin and water; let stand about 4 minutes or until gelatin dissolves. Put egg yolks in processor using steel blade; process until well blended. With processor on add sugar, vanilla and softened gelatin through feed tube. Continue processing and add hot milk and chocolate. Return mixture to saucepan and cook 2 or 3 minutes, stirring constantly. Strain through sieve, cool. Fold in 1 cup of the crème fraîche. Pour into a 3-cup mold that has been rinsed with water. Refrigerate until set. Sprinkle confectioners' sugar over remaining cream; let stand 5 to 10 minutes; fold in. Put cream in pastry bag using star point. Dip mold in hot water for a few moments; dry and invert onto serving dish. Decorate with the sweetened crème fraîche.

BAVAROIS AUX ABRICOTS
Apricot Bavarian Cream
Serves 8

16 large dried apricots
1/2 cup apricot liqueur
1 package unflavored gelatin
1/4 cup cold water
1 cup milk
4 egg yolks
1/2 cup sugar
1/4 cup fresh lemon juice
1 cup heavy cream
7 egg whites
1/2 cup crushed macaroon crumbs
Additional whipped cream

In small bowl cover apricots with water; soak for 12 hours; drain. Put apricots and liqueur in processor using steel blade; process until smooth. Spoon into bowl and set aside. Sprinkle gelatin over water to soften. Heat milk but do not let boil. Put egg yolks in processor using steel blade. With processor on add sugar through feed tube; then add hot milk. Return mixture to saucepan; cook, stirring constantly, until thick and creamy, being careful not to boil. Remove from heat, add gelatin and stir until completely dissolved; cool. Add apricot mixture and lemon juice to custard. Refrigerate until it just begins to thicken.

Whip cream until thick but not stiff and fold into custard mixture. Refrigerate until mixture begins to set. Beat egg whites until stiff; gently fold into custard. Spoon into a lightly buttered 2-quart soufflé dish with collar (see below). Chill at least 3 hours. Remove collar before serving and pat the crushed macaroon crumbs on the exposed sides. Decorate the top with rosettes of whipped cream.

Soufflé collar Measure a strip of aluminum foil or wax paper that will circle the soufflé dish and lap over. Fold the foil lengthwise into thirds. Butter one side. Fit around dish, buttered side in, to make a collar standing 3 inches above the top. Secure with string.

BAVAROIS AUX FRAMBOISES
Raspberry Bavarian Cream
Serves 8

This Bavarian Cream is a delicate pink. Syrup drained from the raspberries is used as a sauce to spoon over the individual servings.

2 10-ounce packages frozen raspberries, thawed
4 eggs, separated
1/2 cup sugar
1 package unflavored gelatin
1/4 cup raspberry syrup or water
1-1/2 cups heavy cream
Dash of cream of tartar
Confectioners' sugar

Drain thawed fruit, reserving syrup. Put fruit in processor using steel blade, process until puréed. Pour fruit into measuring cup, adding syrup, if necessary, to make 1 cup. Put egg yolks in processor using steel blade. With processor on add sugar through feed tube. Add puréed fruit. Pour mixture into bowl and place bowl over saucepan containing gently boiling water. Use a whisk and whisk constantly until thick, about 15 minutes. Dissolve gelatin in 1/4 cup raspberry syrup (or use water if amount is inadequate); add. Whisk mixture over ice cubes until it begins to thicken, or place in refrigerator and whisk frequently.

Whip 1 cup of the cream until slightly thickened; fold into raspberry mixture. Beat egg whites until frothy; add cream of tartar; beat until stiff. Fold into custard. Turn all into a well-buttered 1-1/2-quart soufflé dish fitted with a collar (see preceding recipe). Refrigerate until set. Remove collar. Whip remaining 1/2 cup cream; sweeten to taste with confectioners' sugar. Use to decorate soufflé. Serve remaining raspberry syrup as a sauce.

COEUR À LA CRÈME
Heart of Cream
Serves 8

Light in texture and a very satisfying dessert, Coeur à la Crème is especially attractive when decorated with whole fresh strawberries.

8 ounces cream cheese
1/2 cup confectioners' sugar
Seeds of 1/2 vanilla bean or 1 teaspoon
    vanilla extract
2 cups heavy cream

Sauce aux Fraises (Strawberry Sauce)
1 10-ounce package frozen strawberries,
    thawed and drained
1/2 cup red currant jelly
1 tablespoon Grand Marnier
1 cup fresh strawberries, capped

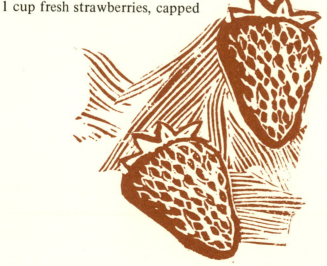

Have cream cheese at room temperature. Put in processor along with sugar, vanilla and 3 table-spoons of the cream, using steel blade. Process until blended and smooth, scraping cheese from sides of bowl with rubber spatula, if necessary. Transfer to large bowl. Whip cream until thick but not stiff; fold into cheese mixture. Cut a large square of cheesecloth; dip in cold water and squeeze out. Line a 4-cup heart-shaped mold or eight individual heart-shaped molds with cheese-cloth or plastic wrap. Fill with cream mixture and fold ends of cloth over top. Refrigerate overnight.

Just before serving time, make sauce. Put thawed strawberries, jelly and Grand Marnier in processor using steel blade. Process until smooth. Unmold cream on platter, remove cloth or plastic. Arrange fresh berries on top of and around mold. Pour some sauce over, serve remaining sauce in bowl. Makes about 1-1/2 cups of sauce.

Note To make sauce with fresh berries, use about 1 basket capped berries. Process with jelly and liqueur as for frozen berries.

MOUSSE AU CHOCOLAT I
Chocolate Mousse I
Serves 6 to 7

6 ounces (squares) semisweet chocolate
1/4 cup rum or strong coffee
1/4 cup toasted blanched almonds
1/4 pound butter
1/4 cup confectioners' sugar
2 eggs, separated
1-1/2 cups heavy cream
3 tablespoons confectioners' sugar
1/2 teaspoon vanilla extract

Combine chocolate and rum in bowl. Place bowl over simmering water; stir frequently until chocolate melts. Remove from heat, let cool but do not allow to set. Turn on processor using steel blade; add almonds through feed tube. Process until ground; remove. Put butter in processor using steel blade. With processor on add the 1/4 cup sugar, egg yolks, melted chocolate and almonds through feed tube. Remove to a large bowl. Whip cream until it begins to form soft peaks; continue beating and add the 3 tablespoons sugar and the vanilla. Spoon out and reserve about 2/3 cup of cream to use for decorating finished mold. Beat egg whites until they form soft peaks. Fold a small amount of whipped cream into chocolate mixture to lighten it. Then fold in remaining cream and egg whites. (If chocolate mixture refuses to blend in smoothly, use mixer and beat at slow speed.)

Line bottom of an 8-inch springform pan with wax paper. (A regular 8-inch cake pan can be used. Line bottom and sides with plastic wrap.) Pour mousse mixture in, cover with plastic wrap and chill in refrigerator 4 to 6 hours. To remove from springform run a knife between mold and pan; unmold and invert on serving platter. Remove bottom and wax paper. To remove from cake pan, invert on platter and remove plastic wrap. Put remaining whipped cream in pastry bag and pipe cream on outer edge of mousse. Make a rosette of cream in center. To serve, cut into wedges.

MOUSSE AU CHOCOLAT II
Chocolate Mousse II
Serves 4

3 ounces (squares) semisweet chocolate
3 tablespoons strong coffee
3 eggs, separated
6 tablespoons sugar
1/2 cup sweetened whipped cream

Put chocolate and coffee in bowl; set over hot water and stir frequently until chocolate melts; let cool. Put egg yolks in processor using steel blade. Process until yolks are light yellow. With processor on add cooled chocolate; transfer to large bowl. Beat egg whites until they form soft peaks; continue beating and gradually add sugar. Beat until whites hold firm peaks. Fold whites into chocolate mixture. Spoon into sherbet dishes. Chill 4 hours or overnight. Decorate with whipped cream.

Sauces

SAUCE DEMI-GLACE
Basic Brown Sauce
Makes about 2-1/2 cups

2 cloves garlic
2 onions
2 carrots
4 tablespoons butter
1 teaspoon sugar
3 tablespoons flour
3 cups chicken stock, see Basics
1 bay leaf
3 sprigs parsley
1 tablespoon tomato paste
1/2 teaspoon salt
1/8 teaspoon black pepper

Put garlic in processor using steel blade. Process until fine, remove. Cut onions in quarters and carrots into 2-inch lengths; put in processor and process until coarsely chopped. Sauté garlic, onions and carrots in butter for about 10 minutes. Add sugar and cook 10 minutes longer, increasing heat so vegetables caramelize and stirring almost constantly to prevent burning. Stir in flour; stir and cook for about 3 minutes. (Flour should be light brown.) Add stock, bay leaf, parsley, tomato paste, salt and pepper. Stir thoroughly. Bring to boil, reduce heat, set lid askew and simmer about 1 hour. Strain.

SAUCES BLANCS
Basic White Sauces

Béchamel and Velouté are the base not only for countless classic French sauces—mornay, suprême, parisienne—but also are the starting point for cream soups and soufflés. By themselves, they are used to accompany egg, fish, chicken, veal and vegetable dishes. Both use a roux of flour and butter; Béchamel is moistened with milk, Velouté with a white stock.

Béchamel Sauce
4 tablespoons butter
4 tablespoons flour
2 cups milk
1/2 teaspoon salt
1/8 teaspoon white pepper

Melt butter in a saucepan. Stir in flour and cook 2 minutes. Add milk; blend well. Stir and cook till thickened. Add salt and pepper. If not using immediately, cover surface with a thin layer of butter or plastic wrap. Makes 2 cups of sauce.

Velouté Sauce Proceed as for Béchamel, above, substituting 2 cups white chicken, veal or fish stock (see Basics). Makes 2 cups of sauce.

SAUCE HOLLANDAISE
Makes about 1 cup

2 egg yolks
1 tablespoon cold water
1/8 teaspoon salt
Dash of white pepper
3/4 cup hot melted butter
1 tablespoon fresh lemon juice

Put egg yolks, water, salt and pepper in processor using plastic blade. Process until yolks are light yellow and airy. With processor still on, add hot butter in a slow, steady stream. Add lemon juice and taste for seasoning. Sauce may be made in advance and kept warm in a water bath; if it separates, whisk in a tablespoon of cold water. For best results prepare just before serving.

Hollandaise Chantilly (Hollandaise with Soured Cream) Add 2 tablespoons crème fraîche (see Basics) to Hollandaise, above. For vegetables.

Hollandaise aux Câpres (Hollandaise with Capers) Wash 2 tablespoons capers in cold water. Drain and dry on paper towels. Coarsely chop in processor using steel blade; add to Hollandaise, above. For eggs, fish and poultry.

Mousseline (Hollandaise with Cream and Egg White) Fold into Hollandaise, above, 1/4 cup whipped cream and 1 stiffly beaten egg white. Taste for seasoning. For vegetables.

SAUCE BÉARNAISE
Makes about 3/4 cup

Excellent for steaks, broiled and fried fish.

2 shallots
3 black peppercorns
1 teaspoon tarragon
4 tablespoons dry white wine or white wine vinegar
2 egg yolks
1 tablespoon cold water
1/8 teaspoon salt
Dash of white pepper
2/3 cup hot melted butter

Put shallots and peppercorns in processor using steel blade. Process until finely chopped. Put into small saucepan with tarragon and wine or wine vinegar. Simmer until liquid is reduced to 2 tablespoons; strain. Put egg yolks, water, salt and pepper in processor using plastic blade. Process until yolks are light yellow and airy. Add hot butter in a slow, steady stream. Add wine mixture and taste for seasoning. Keep sauce warm by setting pan in bowl of warm water. For best results prepare sauce just before serving.

MAYONNAISE
Makes 2-1/2 cups

2 eggs
1/2 teaspoon salt
1/2 teaspoon dry mustard
1/2 teaspoon paprika
2 cups vegetable or corn oil
3 tablespoons fresh lemon juice

Put eggs in processor using plastic blade. Process until eggs are light yellow and airy. With processor on add salt, mustard and paprika. Add 1 cup of the oil in a slow, steady stream; process until thick. Continue processing and add lemon juice; then slowly pour in remaining 1 cup oil. Use immediately or transfer to jar, cover and refrigerate.

MAYONNAISE NOISETTE
Almond Mayonnaise
Makes about 1-1/4 cups

Very good with green beans.

1/4 cup toasted blanched almonds
1 egg
1/4 teaspoon salt
1 cup vegetable or corn oil
2 tablespoons white wine vinegar

Turn processor on using steel blade; add almonds through feed tube. Process until almonds are finely ground; remove steel blade, insert plastic blade. (Do not remove almonds.) Add egg and salt; process until egg is light yellow and airy. With processor on add oil in a slow, steady stream. When mixture thickens, add vinegar. Use immediately or transfer to jar, cover and refrigerate.

MAYONNAISE CHANTILLY
Mayonnaise and Whipped Cream
Makes about 1-1/3 cups

Very good with broccoli or asparagus.

2 eggs
1/4 teaspoon salt
1/8 teaspoon white pepper
1/2 teaspoon paprika
1 cup vegetable or corn oil
3 tablespoons fresh lemon juice
1 tablespoon sour cream or crème fraîche,
    see Basics
1/4 cup whipped cream

Put eggs, salt, pepper and paprika in processor using plastic blade. Process until eggs are light yellow and airy (about 10 to 15 seconds). With processor on add oil in a slow, steady stream. When mixture becomes thick add lemon juice. Pour mayonnaise into bowl; fold in creams.

MAYONNAISE VERTE
Green Mayonnaise
Makes about 2 cups

Good for hors d'oeuvres, eggs, fish and meats.

1 shallot
8 leaves spinach
10 sprigs parsley
1/4 cup watercress leaves, if available
1 cup boiling water
2 eggs
1/2 teaspoon salt
1/8 teaspoon white pepper
1-3/4 cups vegetable or corn oil
2 tablespoons white wine vinegar

Put shallot in processor using steel blade; process until finely chopped; remove. Add shallot, spinach, parsley and watercress to boiling water. Boil for 4 minutes, drain, rinse with cold water, and dry on paper towels. Put green mixture in processor using steel blade; process until puréed; remove. Replace steel blade with plastic blade. Add eggs, salt and pepper; process until eggs are light and airy. With processor on add 1 cup of the oil in a slow, steady stream. When mixture becomes thick add vinegar and remaining oil. Add purée mixture. Use immediately or transfer to jar, cover and refrigerate.

MAYONNAISE AIOLI
Garlic Mayonnaise
Makes 2 cups

Good with cold meats and for hors d'oeuvres.

3 cloves garlic
2 eggs
1/2 teaspoon dry mustard
1/2 teaspoon salt
1-3/4 cups vegetable or corn oil
2 tablespoons wine vinegar

Put garlic in processor using steel blade; process until finely chopped. Remove steel blade, insert plastic blade. (Do not remove garlic.) Add eggs and process until light yellow and airy (10 to 15 seconds). With processor on add mustard, salt and 1 cup of the oil in a slow, steady stream. When mixture becomes thick add vinegar and remaining oil. Use immediately or transfer to jar, cover and refrigerate.

SAUCE VINAIGRETTE
Oil and Vinegar Dressing
Makes 2/3 cup

1 small shallot
2 sprigs parsley
1 teaspoon salt
Dash of black pepper
1/2 teaspoon dry mustard
3 tablespoons white wine vinegar
6 tablespoons vegetable oil or olive oil

Put shallot and parsley in processor using steel blade. Process until finely chopped. Add remaining ingredients and process for a few seconds.

Note A small peeled clove of garlic may be added after processing. Let marinate 30 minutes, remove and discard.

Basics

BOUILLON
Beef Stock
Makes 2 or 3 quarts

1 pound stewing beef
1 pound raw beef bones
1 pound raw veal bones
2 stalks celery
2 carrots
2 medium onions
2 sprigs parsley
1 bay leaf
1 sprig thyme or 1/4 teaspoon dry thyme

Put meat in saucepan. If you buy bones for your stock ask the butcher to cut them into 3- or 4-inch lengths. Add bones to meat and add water to cover by 2 inches. Bring to simmer and remove scum with a spoon. Slice celery, carrots and onions in processor using slicing disc. When scum ceases to appear (this may take 5 minutes) add remaining ingredients and simmer uncovered 3 to 4 hours. Skim when necessary. Add more water when necessary to keep water 1 inch above ingredients. If desired, stew meat may be removed when it is tender, after 1 to 1-1/2 hours of cooking. Meat left in pot the total cooking time becomes tasteless and stringy. At end of cooking time strain stock; taste for strength. If flavor is weak, boil longer to evaporate some of the water content.

Cool stock; set in refrigerator uncovered. When fat hardens, remove and discard. Stock will keep in refrigerator, covered, for a week or more but must be brought to boil every 3 to 4 days. Stock may be frozen in 1- or 2-cup capacity plastic containers. Leave in containers or remove when frozen and put in plastic bags.

FONDS BLANC DE VOLAILLE
Chicken Stock
Makes 2 to 3 quarts

1 whole or half stewing hen
1 pound uncooked chicken bones and skin
    (see note)
1 stalk celery
1 carrot
2 medium onions
1 veal knuckle
2 sprigs parsley
1 bay leaf
1 sprig thyme or 1/4 teaspoon dry thyme
1-1/2 teaspoons salt

Place stewing hen and chicken bones in large saucepan. Add enough water to cover by 2 inches. Bring to simmer. Scum will begin to rise; remove it with a spoon. Continue to remove scum until it ceases to appear. (This may take about 5 minutes.) Slice celery, carrot and onion in processor using slicing disc; add along with remaining ingredients. Partially cover and simmer 2 hours. Add more water when necessary to keep water about 1 inch above ingredients. Remove stewing hen when meat is tender, 1 to 1-1/2 hours. (Reserve meat for use in other recipes.) Continue simmering but do not completely cover until after stock is cool. Do not boil. At end of cooking time, strain and cool stock. Put in refrigerator uncovered and when cold remove hardened fat. Cover stock and keep in refrigerator 7 to 10 days. It must be brought to a boil every 3 to 4 days. Stock may be frozen in 1- or 2-cup capacity plastic containers. Leave in containers or remove when frozen and put in plastic bags.

Note Save bones when you debone chicken breasts or a whole chicken; keep in freezer. Or buy chicken backs.

FONDS BLANC DE VOLAILLE RAPIDE
Quick Chicken Stock
Makes 1 cup

1/2 carrot
1/4 medium onion
1 10-ounce can chicken broth
1/2 bay leaf
1 sprig parsley

Cut carrot into 2-inch lengths, put with onion in processor using steel blade. Process until coarsely chopped. Combine carrot, onion, broth, bay leaf and parsley in saucepan. Simmer 15 to 20 minutes, strain.

FUMET DE POISSON
Fish Stock
Makes 2 to 3 quarts

2 to 3 pounds fish heads, bones and trimmings
   (see note)
1 or 2 fillets fresh flounder or other lean fish
1 onion
8 sprigs parsley
1 teaspoon fresh lemon juice
1/4 teaspoon salt
1 cup dry white wine, optional

Put trimmings and fish in large saucepan. Cut onion in half; slice in processor using slicing disc. Add onion and remaining ingredients to saucepan; add cold water to cover. Bring to simmer, skim; simmer uncovered 30 minutes. Strain through fine sieve. Let cool; store in refrigerator or freeze. Stock may be frozen in 1- and 2-cup quantities in plastic containers. Keep in containers or remove when frozen and put in plastic bags. Stock will keep in refrigerator, covered, for a week or more, but must be boiled every 2 days to keep it from souring.

Note Ask your local fish market to save trimmings for you. Most markets will be glad to do this but you will need to give them several days notice.

FROMAGE PARMESAN RAPÉ
Grated Parmesan Cheese

With a processor in your kitchen it is simple to grate your own Parmesan cheese. Fresh cheese grated at home has far more flavor and aroma than cheese which is purchased in pregrated form.

   Cut Parmesan cheese into pieces 2 or 3 inches wide. Start processor using steel blade, add cheese through feed tube. Process until cheese is very finely grated. Store in jar with lid. Keep in refrigerator. A 5-ounce wedge makes 1-1/4 cups grated cheese.

CHAPELURE
Bread Crumbs

Place any leftover bread in 250° oven until completely dry—perhaps 1 hour. Break bread up, put in processor using steel blade. Process until fine. Store in jar with tight-fitting lid. Will keep almost indefinitely.

Note For fresh, soft bread crumbs, make only as much as will be used immediately. Do not dry bread in oven. Break bread up and process as above.

BEURRE MANIÉ
Butter and Flour Paste
Makes 1 cup

Beurre manié is a good, convenient thickening paste. It always produces a smooth sauce.

1/2 pound butter
1 cup flour

Cut butter into 1- or 2-tablespoon-size pieces. Put butter and flour in processor using steel blade. Process until thoroughly blended and mixture forms a ball. Transfer to bowl, cover and refrigerate. It is very convenient to freeze this paste in tablespoon amounts. When needed, simply add the frozen paste directly to hot liquid and stir and cook until it is dissolved and the sauce is thickened to the desired consistency. The sauce will thicken without lumping. One tablespoon beurre manié will thicken about 3/4 cup of liquid.

BEURRE CLARIFIÉ
Clarified Butter

Cut butter into pieces; place in saucepan and heat on moderate heat. When butter has melted skim off foam and discard. Spoon clear yellow liquid into measuring cup or bowl. Leave milky residue in bottom of pan. The clear liquid is clarified butter. It can be heated to a higher temperature before burning than unclarified butter. Store in jar with lid and refrigerate; will keep several weeks. One-half pound butter makes about 3/4 cup clarified butter.

CRÈME FRAÎCHE
Soured Cream
Makes 2 cups

This crème fraîche is the American version of the commercial French product. In making your own, use a cream with at least 30 percent butterfat.

2 cups heavy cream
2 tablespoons buttermilk

Combine cream and buttermilk. Put in loosely covered jar; let stand at room temperature (not over 85°) until thick. This will take 24 to 48 hours. Cover and refrigerate; will keep 10 days.

Index

ENGLISH INDEX

Almond
  Cake, Chocolate, 93
  Cream, Chocolate, 118
  Custard, 108
  Custard Crêpes, 108
  Mayonnaise, 129
Apple
  Crêpes, 107
  Custard with Meringue, 111
  Mold with Caramel, 110
  Tart, 116
Apricot
  Bavarian Cream, 122
  Glaze, 95, 98-99, 100

Bacon and Onion Pie, 17
Basque Cake, 94
Bass, Whole Striped, in Crust, 33
Bavarian Creams
  Apricot, 122
  Chocolate, 121
  Raspberry, 123
Beans, Green
  and Onions, 80
  Purée, 80
Bean Soup, 23
Béarnaise Sauce, 128
Béchamel Sauce, 127
Beef
  Braised, in Aspic, 61
  Braised, in Beer, 66
  Braised in Red Wine, 60
  Casserole of, with Wine and Olives, 62
  Eye of Round Roast with Vegetables, 63
  Roast, in Wine, 59
  Rolls, Bread-Stuffed, 65

Rolls, Pork-Stuffed, 64-65
Steak Tartar, 12
Stew in Red Wine, 59
Stock, 133
Tenderloin in Puff Pastry, 68
  with Oysters and Mushrooms, 67
Beurre Manié, 136
Bisque, Chilled Salmon, 25
Bread Crumbs, 135
Bread, Rich Yeast, 89
Brioche, 89
Broccoli, Puréed, 79
Brown Sauce
  Basic, 127
  Peppery, 51
Butter and Flour Paste, 136
Butter, Clarified, 136
Butter Cream, 95, 96
  Chocolate, 93
Butter Spongecake, 95

Cabbage
  Green, 82
  Red, Pork Chops with, 74
Cakes
  Basque, 94
  Butter Spongecake, 95
  Chocolate Almond, 93
  Meringue, 96
  Rum Cake Ring, 100-101
  Rum Raisin Cakes, 98-99
  Simple Chocolate, 92
Carrots
  Glazed, 82
  Loaf, 83
  Soup, 21

Chantilly Swans, 104-105
Chestnuts and Whipped Cream, 112
Chicken
  Breasts with Cream Sauce, 47
  Breasts with Mushroom Sauce, 48
  Breasts with Parmesan Cheese, 46
  Cooked in Wine, 50
  Crêpes, 45
  Pork, Wine, Liver and, in Pastry, 76-77
  Roast, 52
  Stock, 134
  Stock, Quick, 134
  Stuffed with Livers, 51
  with Cream, 49
  with Veal Dumplings, 54-55
Chicken Liver Pâté, 13
Chocolate
  Almond Cake, 93
  Almond Cream, 118
  Bavarian Cream, 121
  Butter Cream, 93
  Cake, Simple, 92
  Mousse, I, II, 125
  Sauce, 103
Clarified Butter, 136
Cookies, Rolled, 105
Crab-filled Puffs, 14-15
Crab Meat Filling
  for Cream Puffs, 15
  Soufflé Roll with, 36
Cream, Heart of, 124
Cream Puffs
  Crab-filled, 14-15
  Miniature, 102-103
Cream, Soured, 136
Crème Fraîche, 136

FRENCH INDEX

Biographical Notes

RUTH HOWSE has been professionally involved with cooking since graduating from the University of Tennessee with a bachelor of science degree in home economics. She has taught cooking in Memphis for many years, first on her own 30-minute television show and presently in private classes. She has specialized in teaching French cooking for the past six years, following an intensive study of French cuisine, including classes at the Cordon Bleu and La Varenne cooking schools in Paris. Mrs. Howse has also developed recipes and conducted cooking demonstrations for various food products and appliances. The recipes in this book are those she has used in her classes or served in her home.

RIK OLSON is a free-lance artist/designer/photographer whose many media include a special interest in printmaking. For the illustrations in this book he created an original series of block prints. Rik Olson received his BFA degree from the California College of Arts and Crafts and later spent eight years in Europe as an arts and crafts instructor for the United States Army. While he was abroad, his graphics and photographs were widely exhibited in Germany and Italy, winning a number of awards. Other books he has illustrated include *One Pot Meals* and the Edible Garden Series for 101 Productions.